NATURE'S WAY

.

Nature's Way

A Guide to Green Therapy

TOM GUNNING

BEEHIVE

Published 2022 by
Beehive Books
7–8 Lower Abbey Street
Dublin 1
info@beehivebooks.ie
www.beehivebooks.ie

Beehive Books is an imprint of Veritas
Publications.

ISBN 978 1 80097 006 9

10 9 8 7 6 5 4 3 2 1

Photos on pp. 46 and 110 taken from
iStockphoto.com. All other photos from
the Parable Garden, Ballinesker, Wexford,
www.parablegarden.ie © Tom Gunning,
2022.

Excerpts on pp. 12 and 13 from 'Canal
Bank Walk' by Patrick Kavanagh, from
Collected Poems, Antoinette Quinn (ed.),
Allen Lane, 2004, p. 224, reprinted by
kind permission of the Trustees of the
Estate of the late Katherine B. Kavanagh,
through the Jonathan Williams Literary
Agency; excerpt on p. 29 from 'The
Second Coming' by WB Yeats, from
The Collected Poems of WB Yeats, UK:
Wordsworth Poetry Library, 1994, p.
158; excerpt on p. 41 from 'Blackberry-
Picking' by Seamus Heaney, from *Open
Ground*, London: Faber and Faber Ltd,
2002. By permission; excerpt on p. 71
from *The Sun and Her Flowers* by Rupi
Kaur, London: Simon & Schuster UK,
2017. By permission.

The resources in this book should not be
used to replace the specialised training and
professional judgement of a healthcare or
mental-healthcare professional. Please
always consult a trained professional
before making any decision regarding
treatment of yourself or others.

A catalogue record for this book is
available from the British Library.

Designed and typeset by Padraig
McCormack, Beehive Books
Printed in the Republic of Ireland by
Walsh Colour Print, Kerry

Beehive Books is a member of Publishing
Ireland.

*Beehive books are printed on paper made
from the wood pulp of managed forests. For
every tree felled, at least one tree is planted,
thereby renewing natural resources.*

The breeze at dawn has
secrets to tell you.
Don't go back to sleep.

Rumi

Contents

Introduction

It is now accepted that this generation and those to come will have to fight to save this planet. It has been our only home and the indications from space travel and exploration are that there will be no viable 'planet B' for quite some time. This is our home and this is our only home. As a home provider, it has given us shelter, stability, food and water. Yet recent scientific studies that have emerged over the past few decades have shed a whole new light on the extent to which Mother Nature is nurturing us and caring for us. Her care exceeds food, water and shelter and reaches into such physiological issues as strengthening our immune system, fighting against cancer and helping us to cope with rising levels of depression, stress and anxiety.

There is nothing novel in stating that nature is good for us but it is only recently that it has emerged that our woodlands are green pharmacies that offer free prescriptions to those who are willing to spend a generous amount of time there. It is only in recent times that a view of greenery from a hospital window has been proven to speed up healing whilst also reducing the required level of painkillers. City dwellers who look out on greenery have lower levels of stress and depression along with a heightened sense of well-being and vitality. Nature is now being used to treat PTSD along with ADHD. Doctors in Finland and Japan now offer 'green prescriptions' for remedies for chronic stress and fatigue amongst other maladies.

Nature is now known to repair, restore and renew depleted human physiological systems. It works on the emotional, mental, energetic and spiritual levels as it balances, grounds and teaches. The wide-open spaces at our doorsteps are perfect for self-regulation amidst the growing pressures of consumerism, our increasing workload and the ill effects of screen time. Nature is free, it is varied and, unlike many counsellors and therapists, it is immune to burnout. As long as we don't completely destroy it, it is an inexhaustible and trustworthy therapist, free from judgement or condemnation. It simply heals without asking questions or seeking answers. We don't have to engage in talk therapy when silence and simple acceptance are amongst its most powerful tools. Nature can't cure us of everything and we will always need health professionals and qualified therapists to help us through our challenges, but it is a layer of healing balm that doesn't require payment or an arranged appointment.

In 2016 we created the Parable Garden Education Project in Ballinesker, Co. Wexford. It is located within two walled gardens, adjacent to the wonderful sandy beaches that define that part of the Wexford coastline. The gardens are surrounded by marsh and woodland, wilderness and wildflower meadows. Once opened, we provided courses in ecology and creativity, meditation and Celtic spirituality. It was intended to offer a space to people for education, reflection and experience. Yet from early on it was evident that the most powerful resource was the location itself, the natural green surroundings, the contrast of wilderness and cultivated gardens. More and more we began to rely on nature as the best provider of rest and relaxation, creativity and renewal. Personal experiences of regeneration and the restoration of mind, body and spirit led us to explore the myriad possibilities that the woods and meadows could provide for our participants. In 2018 we created a special area at the edge of our woodland adjacent to the marsh for green therapy. We created small 'cells' hewn from the natural topography where people could rest in nature, free from the pressures of daily living and the noise and hum of everyday life. Our green therapy clinic was born and the next few years were given over to an exploration

> The word 'cell' refers to the small habitable stone buildings that hermits and monks once lived in. They were designed for a solitary lifestyle, free from the distractions of the outside world. They were often located in the grounds of monasteries. Our cells are simpler spaces defined by nature herself.

of the power of nature to act as a teacher, therapist and healer. It is why this book was written.

This book does not seek to challenge any medical or therapeutic services currently available and if a person has medical symptoms they should first consult their own medical practitioner. We are biological and psychological beings who get damaged by the demands and dangers embedded in modern life but this book will point to the growing body of scientific research which shows us that there are healing spaces in our forests, parks and meadows that are somehow fashioned to remedy our ills. Perhaps only the reader can answer the question of whether it is accidental that nature can cure us or it is the result of some grand evolutionary relationship. Research shows that there is a significant percentage of us who actually hate being out in nature and covet instead the great indoors, which, needless to say, diminishes the audience for this book somewhat.

Yet there are many amongst us who completely concur with Patrick Kavanagh's poetic vision: 'Leafy-with-love banks and the green waters of the canal | Pouring redemption for me.' Perhaps scientific research is now catching up on the poetic insight that flowing water and greenery offer a compassionate healing to those who have time to sit and pause, see and listen. So, if you're in any way unwell, consult your trusted medical support but when you're on the way to the waiting room consider walking or even parking your car farther away than usual. Pick a tree-lined route or one that traverses a leafy park. Walk slowly, breathe and take in all the sights and sounds around you. If it makes you feel better, don't be surprised; you've just received a free session of green therapy.

To some extent we have become our own zookeepers, caging ourselves indoors. We've replaced birdsong, pine scents and floral patterns for screens and social media platforms. Nature is proven to de-stress us. Screen time is proven to stress us. We need to unlock ourselves from our devises and go barefoot on meadow grass or a forest floor. We need to feel the feelings that come with rest and deep relaxation. We need to teach our bodies that there is another way of being in the world. Research shows that children who learn the benefits of nature tend to live more sustainably and care for the planet. You are not locked in. Open your front door and go outside. Indulge in some self-care and, while you're out there, imagine some ways you can take care of your caregiver.

This book is divided into three parts and at the end of each there is a section on practical tips for green therapy. Even though this work is based on personal experience along with research, it was ultimately written with a very practical purpose in mind: to promote a greater engagement with the great outdoors. The practical tips sections enable the reader to actively get out in nature and apply the insights and research to their own lives. Green therapy is free, easy and readily available and it starts with opening your front door.

PART 1
Walkabout

O unworn world enrapture me, encapture me in a web
Of fabulous grass and eternal voices by a beech.

Patrick Kavanagh, 'Canal Bank Walk'

1. Our Ancient Home

Many of us have our own preferred place in the great outdoors where we go to rest and relax, be renewed or inspired. We all have different reasons why we like nature and we all have different preferences. Nature is multilayered and multifaceted, providing landscapes that range from icy, rocky outcrops to lush tropical oases. Depending on where you grew up, you may or may not prefer your climate of birth. If you were born in Ireland, for example, it is commonplace to spend much of the year in grey overhanging mist. Working far from home over an extended period might make you long for the grey skies of your birth but, if you still live there, you might long for the sultry clear skies of holiday and sunshine destinations. Far away fields seem greener.

Some people prefer woodlands, some people prefer beaches but are humans wired to prefer particular landscapes over others? In the early eighties, an interesting piece of research was conducted to explore our deeper biological preferences. The surprising results offer us an excellent opening into our journey into the health benefits of green therapy. Professor John Flack of the University of Oregon surveyed a random sample of people from the north-eastern parts of the United States and discovered that they had a preference for savannah-type landscapes over ones that they were more familiar with. He repeated the research in 2009 with people who lived in the tropical rainforests of Nigeria. Again, his research pointed out that a vast majority, when shown pictures of various landscapes, favoured the open savannah. Their preference was not for their more familiar forested environs, even though they had never even visited an open and sprawling grassy region. His research seemed to reveal that humans, in completely different regions of the planet, preferred the grassy plains of tropical or subtropical regions.

So there seems to be a preference buried deep in our unconscious mind for a particular type of natural setting, a place where we feel most at home. The World Health Organization reported that in 2008, as a species, the majority of us had moved into urban or city dwellings. This was a first in our history; hitherto we were primarily agricultural or rural dwellers. It was only with modernity and the industrial revolution that we began to migrate to cities and urban centres in search of employment and a better quality of life. Yet what has transpired from research is that we don't thrive in cityscapes. In fact, we're more prone to become stressed and anxious in an urban setting. Quite simply, grey and concrete urban and city environs don't suit our species. We have a preference for natural surroundings and, in particular, the open plains of the savannahs even though most of us have never even lived on them. It is projected that by 2050 over 75 per cent of the earth's population will have migrated to cities. Europeans now spend 90 per cent of their time indoors. While inside, many of us now spend as much time on our screens as we do sleeping.

What we discern to be 'human' is possibly only two hundred thousand years old but we have been evolving over many hundreds of millions of years. Our family tree doesn't begin a couple of hundred thousand years ago. Instead, the tree reaches back into the beginning of the Palaeozoic era when the first animals began to roam around the earth. Their brains formed the basis of the modern central nervous system and, even though we have greatly evolved and developed, the reptilian brain of our primate ancestors still sits right on top of our brainstem, which is the part connected to our spine. This ancient part of our neurological makeup may be called the 'reptilian brain' but it is hugely advanced. We can only come to appreciate why nature is good for us if we first arrive at an understanding of the role of the reptilian brain in the modern world.

This primitive part of our brain takes care of our survival and, therefore, it has to process all of the information coming into our neural circuitry every single second. It never switches off because there is never a time when we might not be damaged by some external animate or inanimate object. The higher and more evolved parts of our brain lie further up in the frontal lobes, just behind our foreheads. Sensory information only arrives at this region after it has first been analysed by the survival region. If an object is falling on top of us, for example, this visual and auditory data will first be processed by the thalamus, which is right behind our nasal area. This is because we can often sniff out danger. The shortest route for incoming data to our brain is from the eyes, ears and nose to the thalamus. It immediately processes all of the information to decide if there is a threat. It is doing this even as you read these lines. It never stops.

If there was a piece of plaster falling from your ceiling, the thalamus would inform the central nervous system to get you out of the way, even before your conscious mind registered it. Your body would have moved milliseconds before you knew the plaster was falling. The reason for this is that it would take too long for all the sensory data to make its way up to your frontal lobes and for you to then 'decide' what to do. So every single piece of data that you perceive from the external world has first been filtered through the survival part of your brain. It has a veto, if you like, on everything that happens to you. It is a rather ingenious system of 'first responders' to all threats and emergencies. The next time you walk down the street and your body pulls you out of the way of an oncoming car before you even see it, thank your reptilian brain. The next time you jump out of your seat when someone drops something in a restaurant, thank (or blame) the oldest regions and circuits of your brain. They are minding us so they never switch off, even when we are sleeping.

These regions are part of our instinctual and intuitive systems and are also linked to our 'gut' feelings. This part of our brain has instantaneous access to all our memories and associations via the hippocampus, and all of this is going on without you even thinking about it. This is because it's all about your survival and it doesn't have time to get 'you' involved in wondering and mulling over what the right option to take is. There are some incredible stories of fire personnel who make decisions to leave burning buildings seconds before they collapse. And it's all based on gut instinct. Afterwards, when asked why they rapidly exited, they actually can't explain it. Yet a probable explanation is that the old brain was swiftly going through all the available data and quickly making decisions based on previous knowledge and experience. This subconscious part of our brain can operate up to six hundred times faster than the conscious mind. We shouldn't take this personally but, when it comes to survival, our conscious minds are just too slow.

Many species have come and gone but we still exist and we can thank the extraordinary way that the brain has structured itself. Even though the brain has evolved many times, it has kept this region active right where it is because it is so crucial to our safety and survival. This is excellent news, that we have such vigilant guardians nestling at the top of our spines but, unfortunately, it does come at a price.

The survival regions do seem to be a bit hypervigilant and overly sensitive. Yes, there are threats to our survival but not that many. For the most part, we live in well-built houses that are secure from intruders. Smoke detectors and carbon-monoxide alarms protect us from various toxins and threats. Roads and speed regulations make crossing the street relatively danger free. Modern cars come with an array of safety features and airbags. A plethora of regulations governs food safety, so the chances of being poisoned in the supermarket are remote. So the question is why does the human brain remain so dependant upon an ancient piece of neural circuitry? Surely at this stage in our technological advancement, hypervigilance has become obsolete?

The answer to this question is yes, it is overly vigilant, but changing the neural makeup of our brain is not as easy as downloading the latest piece of software into your mobile phone. The reality is that changing the software in your phone takes minutes and changing the software in your brain takes about ten thousand years. This is why, even today, humans all over the globe, prefer the look of the savannah to any other landscape. And yes, you probably guessed correctly, your reptilian brain probably made that decision for you because this is where it feels safest.

The Savannahs

When a child is born, its brain does not know what year it is, where it is or who is minding it. Slowly, through a process of nurturing and other experiences, the brain slowly realises where it is, who it is and who its guardians are. The major problem that faces all modern humans is the fact that the primitive brain never really comes to realise that it is living in a relatively safe environment. It doesn't know that it drives around surrounded by airbags and lives behind locked doors. It simply hasn't evolved that way and, as far as it's concerned, it is still living out in nature sometime possibly around eight thousand years ago. The health and safety manual from which it is operating is thousands of years out of date but it doesn't know this. Therefore, the security system in our brain can only adequately cope with the conditions for which it was programmed; in other words, the great outdoors. So, if we feel safer and calmer outside in nature, it is partly because this is where our ancient brain feels safe and at home.

The reptilian brain was still on high alert in its natural surroundings of woodlands, plains, rivers and mountains but at least it was able to cope adequately with the level of threat posed. The significant issue, which we will address in the next chapter, is that the primitive brain is completely out of its depth in a modern urban setting. There is simply too many stimuli and too much data coming at it for it to be able to work out whether there is any danger or not. Constantly overwhelmed, it stresses up and goes into a state of hypervigilance and high alert. This eventually can lead to high levels of stress and anxiety.

Let's imagine for a moment what it was like for the primitive brain in its natural surroundings, many thousands of years ago. Humans lived in caves and natural shelters and roamed in groups of about thirty in order to catch their prey and strip and carve up their kill. There was safety in

Open views, like this one from the top of Holly Hill looking down to Ballinesker beach, were preferred by our ancestors as they could more easily detect a threat from wild animals and other predators.

numbers so the group was close knit, even taking care of the sick and disabled. The main dangers were from predators like sabre-toothed tigers, bears and other animals that might like a human for dinner. The other main threat came from famine or worrying levels of food supplies. These were the two main factors that would have caused the reptilian brain to become alarmed and send signals to the body that there was a threat.

Once the thalamus registers a threat, like being chased by a tiger, the amygdala sends stress chemicals into our bodies via the sympathetic nervous system. Adrenaline gets us to move quickly and stimulates the muscles and skeletal structure to get us to run or fight back. This is known as the fight or flight response. Cortisol gets our brains to think very quickly. It's not a very clear or reflective type of thinking. Instead, it's trying to work out where to run to escape the chasing predator. Rapidly, we were trying to work out whether to turn left or right, go

up a tree or run into a cave. When the sympathetic nervous system is active we become stressed. Stress in itself is not a bad thing; it is the human body's way of getting us out of danger.

Once the threat was passed and we escaped, the parasympathetic nervous system signalled for the brain to stop releasing the stress chemicals. Then a new set of chemicals or neurotransmitters were released, like serotonin or norepinephrine. These signalled for the body to start to rest and recover. Nature was crucial to this whole process of slowing down, resting and recovering. Research shows that it was the visual and aural data from the natural surroundings that helped our ancestors to switch from the stressful state to the relaxed state. So basically, nature helps humans to alleviate stress. The processes that helped the reptilian brain thousands of years ago haven't changed. We still need nature to de-stress and that is as relevant for our contemporaries working in urban centres as it was for our ancestors out on the savannahs. It is to these urban centres and the people who live and work in them that we now turn our attention.

2. Urban Living

We have an inbuilt preference for the savannah-type landscape and some of that comes down to how our visual field works. Visual data makes up about 50 per cent of our brain processing power so we rely on it a lot. That's why when we close our eyes we immediately feel rested, because our brain can shut down a significant amount of neural processing. The primitive brain is always looking out for danger so it is easier to see if there is a threat in the broad open plains of a savannah. We can spot an approaching bear or tiger far easier in open plains than in the cramped conditions of an unfamiliar forest or wooded outcrop. The brain feels safer here and doesn't need to release stress hormones in case something jumps out on us unexpectedly. We can also determine where there is food when we can see into the distance in a broad panoramic sweep. All of nature can act to relieve us of stress but there is a preference for the visual expanse of the open plains.

The reason why green therapy is good for us is because contemporary lifestyles are providing far more sources of stress for our bodies and brains than there were for our primitive ancestors. Our central nervous system is unable to cope with the sheer weight and pace of incoming data. Our ancestors had far fewer stressors but they also had time to allow nature to de-stress them. This is the fascinating finding that is coming out of recent research into the healing benefits of nature; it is nature that tells our systems to de-stress but never before in the history of humanity have we had so little access to it. The World Health Organization now calls stress the epidemic of the twenty-first century.

Too Many Stressors

The amygdala in the brainstem is the key region when it comes to generating fear. Research shows that in urban settings more blood flows to the amygdala, while in natural surroundings blood flows away from it. This suggests that the primitive part of our brain is in a heightened state of alertness when we are in cities or towns. The reason for this is that the features and stimuli in the city are as far away from open plains as one could possibly get. When we visit or live in a city we are not always aware that stress chemicals are being released into our bodies. This all happens at a subconscious level and the reptilian brain is responding to events in a particular way without us actually realising it. If we stopped and checked in with our heart rate and breathing, we might get a sense that we are under pressure but we rarely get a chance to do that in the fast-paced momentum of modern living. In other words, just because we don't feel that something is detrimental to us, doesn't mean it's not. We might be quite happy in the cityscape, looking forward to all the business and activity, but our reptilian brain, which has control over our stress chemicals, is not feeling safe or secure. Blood is flowing to the amygdala and research shows that humans living in cities are more prone to stress, anxiety and depression than their counterparts living in the countryside.

The primitive brain likes there to be as few distractions as possible as it scans the horizon and environment for threats. There are no tigers roaming our cities but the amygdala hasn't evolved to know this. It can relax out in nature because there are fewer distractions and it is the environment that it has evolved to be most familiar with. There were still threats in the forest, but it was a familiar landscape. If our evolution was mapped out over a twenty-four-hour time period, we have literally just moved into cities in the last few milliseconds. The brain adapts and evolves slowly, so it will take time to catch up. The reptilian part of our brain sees lots of cars coming at it but is overwhelmed. There are countless emails, notifications and demands from the modern workplace. There are distractions, stimuli and constant forces vying for our attention. There is simply too much going on for the primitive brain to adequately figure out if there is a tiger lurking somewhere around a corner or not. Whilst we're distracted by all our activities, the amygdala is on high alert and, therefore, starts to release all of the stress chemicals into the central nervous system. Research shows that the low vibration and murmur of urban sounds are sometimes interpreted by the brain as similar to the signals and sounds from a marauding predator. So, the amygdala hears the roar of a tiger, but just can't see it with all of the multiple signals coming from the urban jungle so it stresses up. No matter how advanced we think we are, urban sounds are being picked up as stressors by the sympathetic nervous system.

Green Medicine

The impact of the urban experience on our nervous system is a matter for some concern but the real problem lies in the fact that we no longer have as much access to nature as our ancestors. This is unfortunate because it was the sounds and sights of nature that triggered the brain to switch off the stress chemicals and release the rest and recover hormones and neurotransmitters. So after our ancient uncle successfully escaped the claws of the tiger, he rested up a tree or on a rocky ledge. The shades and patterns of the blues and greens along with the sounds of birds chirping and water softly flowing were the signals to his system to become calm again. Then his lymphatic system could drain off the stress chemicals and restore the body to a state of balance or homeostasis.

The bodies that we live in are not, and never were, designed to be stressed the whole time. Our ancestors might have been stressed two or three times a week at a maximum. They were always on the alert but rarely did the sympathetic nervous system have to activate. Modern men and women unfortunately find themselves in a stressful state quite regularly and over time this drains us mentally, physically and emotionally. We need to find ways to counteract the effects of the multiple stressors we encounter every day from driving a car to screen time and the demands of modern communication systems. Our forebears had access to nature to help them to restore their systems to the relaxed state but unfortunately that is limited for us. The crucial point to remember is that our bodies are designed to be in the rest and digest state more often than the fight or flight state. When we continuously throw ourselves off balance we find ourselves suffering from the multiple effects of chronic or ongoing stress. This is one reason why the study and practice of green therapy is significant: it helps us to mend and heal our bodies from the harmful effects of stressful lifestyles.

It was Roger Ulrich, architect and professor, who first presented research showing how green therapy works. He demonstrated how the sights and sounds of nature activate the healing, balancing and restorative parasympathetic nervous system. Ulrich is one of the pioneer researchers in this area and his work began back in the early eighties when, as an architect and environmental psychologist, he discovered that patients in hospitals who have a room with a view of greenery healed quicker and needed fewer painkillers. He wasn't really the first to discover this; Florence Nightingale was also convinced that being wheeled outdoors led to a quicker recovery.

Ulrich's first study, titled 'View through a window may influence recovery from surgery', in 1984, studied patients in a hospital in Pennsylvania who were recovering from gall-bladder surgery. He studied two different groups of patients. One group looked out onto deciduous trees, while the other looked out onto a brick wall. Those who looked out onto the trees had lower levels of stress, had a more positive outlook and were discharged slightly earlier. Later research carried out in the University of Kansas reported that patients who had flowers or a plant beside their bed suffered from less anxiety and had lower blood pressure.

The idea of green medicine can be traced back to the idea of therapeutic gardens in the early Benedictine monasteries. Here the idea developed that the health and vitality of the human body and

A walled garden is the ideal setting for a therapeutic garden. The sense of a walled enclosure creates a feeling of safety and security that in turn stimulates the parasympathetic nervous system, allowing us to feel rested and at peace.

spirit could somehow be related to the state of the life force of the surrounding natural world. It points to a special connection between humans and the earth that we walk on. The Korean proverb *shin tu bul ee* translates as 'Body and soil are one'. The first human, Adam, was named after the Hebrew *Adamah*, which means 'red earth' or 'soil'. Perhaps if we want to understand the human condition, we should do no more than look down at the ground we walk upon. After all, we are human, from the Latin term *humus* meaning 'earth' or 'ground'. Perhaps that's why we prefer when we're more 'down to earth'.

Many indigenous cultures, in particular, see no distinction between themselves and the natural world around them. It was sometime after the Enlightenment that we began to see ourselves as distinct from the earth but up until then we understood ourselves to be one species among many others. We were part of the earth and the earth was part of us. Just as the human body can heal a part of itself that is sick or damaged, maybe the earth and its lush natural coat of reds, browns and greens can make us feel better too. If we are part of it, instead of separate, then maybe the whole can heal the part that is damaged. In our case, the part that is broken is humanity itself with its modern-day stresses, strains and worries.

Saint Hildegard of Bingen created the term *viriditas,* from the Latin words for 'green' and 'truth'. *Viriditas* was the font and flow of divine healing energy embedded in the natural world. This flow was the origin of all goodness and health. She believed we could benefit from immersing ourselves in nature and eating particular foods that had known healing properties. Many monasteries had medicine gardens full of herbs and shrubs with healing properties. Hildegard believed that we would flourish as long as nature flourished around us. There was a relationship between *human* and *humus,* a resonance between the green vitality in nature and the biological vitality that coursed through our veins.

Modern research methods are now beginning to produce data that backs up Hildegard's *viriditas* maxim, that our health is in some mysterious way linked to the health of the natural world that grows around us. For example, the emerald ash borer is a bug that attacks ash trees and at the turn of the millennium it arrived in North America. Within four years, over a million trees had died in the plague that spread across woodlands, tree-lined parks and urban areas. Then the US Forest Service started researching mortality rates across the counties most affected by the emerald ash borer. They found higher mortality rates in these areas as people were dying with cardiovascular and lower respiratory tract illness. The research pointed to a possible correlation between the health of the forests and the health of the humans that lived in them. So, are our woodlands really that important for our health, and if they are, how can trees heal us? It's time to take a walk in the woods.

3. A Walk in the Woods

Our lives can be viewed as a series of promises that we make or contracts that we sign. These can often be the happiest moments of our lives. The new job, new house or marriage are amongst the most meaningful commitments we ever make. As time wears on, however, even the joyous events of the past can become burdensome. Time tends to wear things and they lose their *viriditas*, for want of a better word. Systems lose their energy, relationships their novelty. As WB Yeats put it, 'Things fall apart; the centre cannot hold.' In Robert Frost's poem 'Stopping by Woods on a Snowy Evening', the horse rider pauses by the woods on the evening of the winter solstice, the darkest day of the year. He wants to stay to watch the woods fill up with snow, except he has promises to keep and miles to go before he sleeps. We have all made these promises and they are the ones that sometimes weigh upon us as we try our best to keep them. When our lives feel like they are wearing thin and the enthusiasm and vitality of the past fades, maybe a trip to the woods can restore something that feels as if it has been lost.

Possibly as Frost's horse rider was gazing into the forest, he felt something of the revitalising flow that comes from our relationship with the natural world, and trees in particular. The Japanese have a special word for this relationship, *yūgen*. It refers to that deep intuition we have in our gut and bones that nature will calm, restore and make us whole again. To be healed is to become whole again. The Japanese have been promoting this restorative relationship with the forest for many years now. The National Institute of Public Health of Japan actively promotes what it refers to as 'forest bathing' or shinrin-yoku. It has become an officially recognised way to prevent disease and promote well-being in Japan. A more accurate translation of *shinrin-yoku* might be 'taking in the forest atmosphere', as it is not really like taking a bath.

Doctor Qing Li, in his book *Shinrin-yoku: The Art and Science of Forest-Bathing*, describes how simply being in nature restores health and happiness. What's notable is that it is not another task to be done, an exercise or practice to master. It would appear that it is ideal for weary, worn out humans because all you need to do is be in nature and connect with it through your senses. It is simply about being really present or fully immersed in its greens and browns, russets, pine scents and birdsong. It is an invitation to be fully immersed in many woodland sensations, as one might be immersed in a lovely scented bath.

In the city, we move around a lot and at a fast pace. It can throw our nervous system out of balance. Yet, in the forest, you'll notice that the trees hardly move at all. They stand still, gently swaying in the breeze like some ancient guardians of calm. Even though it appears that they are doing very little, they somehow get everything done. The Taoist term *Wu wei* refers to effortless effort. It would appear that trees have mastered this. They hardly move, but come summer they will be laden with a canopy of green leaves and will bear untold amounts of seeds to propagate themselves. They do this without seeming to do much at all and in winter deciduous trees close down virtually all their systems. If we can immerse ourselves in the ether of our old forest grandparents, we will be taught a different pace. They will give us permission to slow down and enjoy effortless effort. As Dr Li states, 'When we are in harmony with the natural world we can begin to heal. Our nervous system can rest itself, our bodies and minds can go back to how they ought to be.'

In the Japanese forests, cedar trees have grown for over a thousand years and some rainforests have been left untouched for many thousands of years. These forests are thought to be sacred and in

Shintoism the spirits, or *kami,* live in nature, in the cypress trees, rocks and rivers. They are the sacred spaces of spiritual renewal and the Japanese believe that we are all in need of such shrines. A huge percentage of Japanese people live in cramped cities and are constantly jammed into early morning subways. The term *tsukin jigoku* describes their 'commuter hell'. The Japanese also suffer from a phenomenon known as *karoshi,* or 'death from overwork'. The term 'technostress' describes the burden that technology now places on our systems and it can lead to anxiety, depression, insomnia and fatigue. We have all been attracted to the bright lights of the city but sometimes the razzle-dazzle just bedazzles us.

It was in the context of the rigours of urban living that in 1982 shinrin-yoku became a national health programme in Japan. Something was needed to rebalance a worn-out workforce and, thankfully, it was freely available in the local forests. Doctor Li draws upon a wealth of data and research that shows that spending time in a forest can:

- Reduce blood pressure
- Lower stress
- Improve cardiovascular and metabolic health
- Lift depression
- Improve pain thresholds
- Increase energy
- Boost the immune system
- Increase anti-cancer protein production
- Help in weight loss

Over the course of the next few chapters we will be exploring the health benefits of being in nature in greater depth because once we know why and how therapy can work for us, we might be likely to spend more time availing of this multicoloured, multilayered healing balm. Forests now can receive certificates in 'green healing'. The first forest to be awarded this accolade in Japan was Iiyama. It was there that Dr Li and his team first did research on levels of human stress in particular. They proved that forest bathing can lower the stress chemicals adrenaline and cortisol

| The Woods at the Parable Garden.

whilst also lowering blood pressure. Time in the forest suppresses the sympathetic nervous system as it enhances the parasympathetic nervous system. In simple terms, in the forest we feel safer, calmer and more balanced.

Annually up to five million people avail of forest bathing in sixty-two certified 'green healing' forests. Doctor Li began by studying the effects of forest bathing on stress but other interesting material showed up with his group of research volunteers. They reported that the length and quality of their sleep was much improved after their trips to the forest at Iiyama. Research shows that a two-hour hike through the forest can increase the length of sleep by up to 15 per cent. Perhaps none of this is surprising. When we spend time in the forest we are soothing and bathing the oldest parts of our brain. The ancient neural structures are lost and on high alert in the cityscape but natural environs feel like home and the Japanese forests have now provided some welcome scientific research to back that up. The stress chemical cortisol interrupts our sleep patterns because the brain doesn't like us sleeping if it feels we are threatened in any way. The presence of this chemical can keep us awake and can even be linked to bad or disturbing dreams. Once the level of this chemical is lowered through forest bathing, the chances of a better night's sleep rise dramatically.

Once we understand the mechanisms behind the release and suppression of the stress chemicals we can begin to appreciate another effect of walking, running or hiking in the forest. When we become stressed, the brain interprets it as a threat that we must escape from. That's why blood flows to the muscular structures during stress. The body literally wants us to move out of the way, to run, flee, escape. If we remain seated in an office all day and we don't walk or run off the stress chemicals, they tend to build up in our bodies. The brain can keep releasing these neurotransmitters because it's getting even more stressed that we're not running or attempting to evade the predator or threat. Walking or hiking in the forest serves to activate the muscular skeleton, which sends signals to the brain that we are 'running away from the threat'. Obviously, there is no tiger to run away from but sometimes it helps to play along with the emotional needs of our older brain.

Serotonin is one of the neurotransmitters that inform the nervous system that we can now relax but, significantly, it is created deep in the brainstem. The primitive brain won't release any more of this chemical unless it is convinced that the threat has passed and we are safe. It has recently come to light that our large leg muscles play a significant role in reducing stress levels because they are sending signals to the brain that we are moving, escaping or attempting to evade the threat. So, when we couple running, walking or movement in general with an immersion in nature, the older brain's preferred home, we can see beneficial effects.

Different trees can have a different symbolic meaning for us. The willow tree has drooping curved branches that allow rain and snowfall to easily fall off. It is designed to let go. Their root system cleanses the run-off water from the fields of all toxins before it enters the sea. Willow bathing invites us to cleanse ourselves of the old, to let go and embrace the new.

Practical Tips

Here are some practical tips on how to get the best out of time spent in nature. Ideally something like forest bathing should last for a couple of hours but in practice the health benefits of being in nature can be felt after fifteen to twenty minutes. Other research suggests that even looking at a plant or picture of nature can have an immediate effect on cognitive ability. Nature never judges us, so it is never about the right amount of time or the wrong amount of time. Also, it is never about the right practice or the performance of a technique. The natural space is always an invitation to just be ourselves and be at rest. More than likely, that's exactly what the plants and animals around you will be doing.

1. Thresholds

According to researchers, one of the most important factors in the health benefits of being in nature is that it acts almost like a refuge or sanctuary from the demands of the ordinary world. The woodland, beach or meadow can act like a ritual space where we separate from the 'ordinary' world and cross a threshold into the 'special' world of healing and renewal. The mind will tend to ruminate and even brood on matters so it is helpful to consciously mark the crossing into nature so as to maximise the benefit and let go of the ordinary stuff of the day.

Physical thresholds allow us to mentally make a crossing from the ordinary world of our daily worries and pressures into the special world of rest, renewal and restoration.

- It is best to mute, switch off or simply leave your phone behind when you immerse yourself in nature. If we are in places that we are familiar with, it might make us feel safer to leave our phones behind. We can only fully relax if we feel safe.
- Consciously mark a spot on a path or at a boundary where you feel you are crossing into a place of healing and renewal. Studies suggest that knowing that nature is good for us enhances the experience.
- Deal with any niggling thoughts before you enter the natural space. Make the phone calls or send the messages that need to be sent so you can leave them behind you.
- Walk into your space slowly, allowing yourself to start paying attention to the new sights, smells and sounds.

2. Slowing Down

It is said that it takes a tree a full eight hours to take an in breath and another eight hours to exhale. Trees don't have lungs but they do take in carbon dioxide and release oxygen. When we are in a forest, the trees breathe in our exhaled breath and we breathe in their exhaled breath. Often when we enter the woods or a park, we have been busy so our walking and breathing might be fast. One of the reasons nature is good for us is because we start to slow down and harmonise ourselves with the slower pace of nature's rhythms.

- After you've crossed your threshold, become aware of the speed of your steps. Nature is never a place of 'having to do' anything. It's about resting, so just observe the speed of your movement.

- Allow your mind to enjoy the feeling that in here there is nothing to be done. This is a place of doing nothing. As your thoughts begin to slow down, allow your body to harmonise with this slower mental activity.

- There is no destination, purpose or thing to be done when our intention is to be healed and renewed by nature. We just need to simply be. Sauntering or ambling along is a good term to describe our more relaxed and rested movements in nature.

- Whenever you come across a suitable space allow yourself to sit down and rest.

3. Sanctuary Space

Environmental psychologists Rachel and Stephen Kaplan, who we'll meet again later in this book, are pioneers in the area of the health benefits of nature. They put forward the idea of finding a 'shed' in the natural world. It is a place that we can become familiar with and most importantly it is a place where we feel safe. The parasympathetic nervous system can only be activated when we feel safe. A 'shed' need not be a physical structure but rather a place where we can see, but not be seen. It is a refuge or a sanctuary space where there are no other humans so there are no demands put on us.

The Viking Seats overlook an area of marsh wilderness, untouched by human hands for hundreds of years.

- A garden shed, tree house or fort is an ideal place to bask in nature. If we use our own property, chances are we'll feel protected and safe.
- Nature provides built-in hiding places that are not too hard to find. Clusters of bushes, long meadow grass and sand dunes all provide purpose-built refuges.
- There is a particular appeal for wilderness areas in nature therapy. Usually they are more remote and less frequented by other people. Familiarity with an area over time will induce feelings of safety.
- Elevated areas are where our ancestors would have sought refuge after an escape or attack. These are ideal vantage points for our systems to be washed with our natural relaxing chemicals.

4. Breathing

There are as many different breathing techniques as there are clouds in the sky. If you have learned a technique that suits you then nature is a good place to practise it. The greatest health benefit of nature is its effect on our central nervous system. The parasympathetic nervous system slowly begins to take over and we feel less stressed and more relaxed. We will notice this change in our breathing. In later chapters we will examine the particular qualities of forest air but for now it's just good to know that the air in woodlands is very beneficial.

- Nature is good for us because it just lets us be ourselves. It has no desires that we need to fulfil or needs that we need to meet. It is inviting us to rest, let go of worries and just breathe. There is no need to think we have to perform a breathing technique that we may get right or may get wrong.
- The body is very intelligent and it will breathe in a nice and relaxed matter once we give it permission. The mind needs to settle first and then the body will slow down. Next we will just witness the body breathe more deeply and more slowly.
- The body will thank us for this moment of rest that we are giving it. It will enjoy breathing the way it wants to, free from stress and demands. So just observe the body enjoying itself.
- Nature's air is full of good things so feel free to take nice long, deep breaths if it feels comfortable. Again, when we know something is good for us, it increases its benefit.

5. Harmonising

The rhythms, movement and pace of nature are much slower, yet everything gets done. Nature never rushes or gets anxious about deadlines. Yet it still provides the entire planet with all its food on a daily basis. That's no small task! We can learn a lot about how to go about our daily business by simply observing the movement and rhythms of nature. In effect, this will allow us to harmonise our rhythms, movement and work with nature's way.

- Nature allows us to slow down and rest so it is natural to feel like we can just close our eyes. As your brain slows down with a break from all the visual data, just allow your body to feel that it's okay to do nothing for a moment or two.
- Birdsong is amongst the most pleasant and relaxing sounds for the parasympathetic nervous system. Simply allow yourself to enjoy the sounds. The birds spend a lot of time just sitting and singing. Yet everything gets done.
- Nature lacks for nothing. A bare patch of ground or soil will become green in a short time. There is an abundance of life, energy and provisions in the natural world. Allow yourself to feel the feeling that there is enough. Allow the thought that you have enough. In that moment, you have everything you need.
- When you open your eyes, observe how slowly everything moves in your natural setting. This slowness is deep therapy for tired minds, muscles and bodies. In order to receive this therapy, all you have to do is do nothing and simply observe. One of the most important forms of therapy we can get is the permission to just do nothing.

PART 2
Senses

Late August, given heavy rain and sun
For a full week, the blackberries would ripen.
At first, just one, a glossy purple clot
Among others, red, green, hard as a knot.
You ate that first one and its flesh was sweet
Like thickened wine: summer's blood was in it

Seamus Heaney, 'Blackberry-Picking'

4. Sights and Sounds

The best way to get the most out of forest bathing is to immerse as many of our senses as we can in the experience. Most of us know that nature is good for us, but in this second part we're going to examine exactly why that is the case. There is a mystery to all of this as well because each individual has their own particular relationship with nature and its relevance and meaning may be beyond linguistic or rational interpretation; however, examining the research around the subject can help us to improve our interaction with nature. When we discover why something is good for us we tend to give it more time or respect it more. The purpose of this book is to encourage the reader to place time with nature high on their list when it comes to self-care, personal growth and simple enjoyment. We have to learn how to let nature take care of us. Sometimes we just have to learn how to get out of our own way, to allow something else to mind us.

When we take a walk in nature or just sit there in her presence, it is not too difficult to appreciate how the sights, sounds and smells in some way are combining to create a restorative experience for us. Nature therapy is a sensory experience and in this chapter we will focus on the visual and aural aspects of green therapy. Remember, it was Roger Ulrich who first reported the healing properties of the sights of greenery and trees; the question we can now ask is what exactly is going on with all of this visual data that is so appealing to us? As we answer this question, we add another layer to our understanding of the healing properties of our natural environment. Its healing balm is multilayered; some of it we will understand, some of it will remain gloriously shrouded in mystery. In the third part of this book, we will explore our relationship with nature as an encounter. If we meet another human being and fall in love with them, we can never fully understand why we fell head over heels. Our most meaningful experiences will always evade the strict analysis of rational and scientific research. Given the choice, we would probably have it no other way.

We have spoken about the possibility of creating thresholds to cross before we go for our forest walk. It enables us to leave behind unwanted thoughts and feelings when we are enjoying ourselves in nature. It is difficult to fully immerse in the forest bathing experience if there is a niggling thought vying for our attention. The entrance to the forest can become a crossing of sorts, a passage into an easier place for the mind, body and soul. It is a stronger signal to the mind if we can visually look at a crossing point. All the great spiritual journeys of the enlightened masters were dotted with crossings of one form or another. They were places to leave the old behind and embrace the new, be it a mountaintop, wilderness or odyssey.

Sights

If we leave behind an urban setting to enter a natural one, our visual field changes completely and this brings about an immediate change in our brain activity. Visually, we have crossed a threshold into something new. Remember, the visual part of our brain takes up a vast amount of computing power so when we alter the visual field it brings a significant change to our internal neural workings. Researchers have been actively studying what exactly it is about nature and its vast array of environs that is so pleasing to the eye. Strangely, it partly comes down to maths and geometrical shapes and patterns. We can never capture exactly why it is we like looking at greenery and woodland pastures but here are some tantalising hints.

Roger Taylor, a professor of physics and biology at the Materials Science Institute in Oregon, has been studying the patterns that can be found in nature and their effect on us. He has discovered particular designs in trees that can be termed 'fractal patterning'. A fractal is a repeated pattern in a structure from its macro to its microelements. Take, for example, the crystal in a snowflake. The arrangement and pattern of the crystal is repeated over and over again no matter how far we zoom in on the microscope. If we look at trees, the shape of the trunk and its relationship to the branch is repeated geometrically when we examine the relationship of the branch to a smaller branch or twig. The same fractal patterning can be seen in the veins of a leaf. You can see this yourself if you pick up a fern or leaf. Its design remains constant as you peer deeper and deeper into its substructures. The same fractal patterning can be observed in the root system of a tree. It would appear that humans are programmed to like fractal designs and their predictability.

When we look at any object, person or landscape the brain only processes a small fraction of the visual field. The rest is guesswork based on previous experience. It just takes too much computing power to process all the optic data. Fractal patterning makes the brain's work much easier due to the amount of repeated identical patterns. The brain can easily process the data because it's just the same repeated design all over again. Professor Taylor also did experiments with an eye-tracking machine; he tracked the retinal movements of the eye when looking at artworks and other objects. The eye used a search pattern that was itself fractal. First it scanned the macro image and then began to explore the micro images but in a repeated fashion as if it were looking for fractals. Some artists, such as Jackson Pollock, use fractals in their paintings and this is why many people find their work so pleasing to the eye. When some animals are tracked as they search for food, their routes and tracks follow fractal patterns; so it would appear that it is also an efficient way to hunt.

The golden mean or golden ration is also present in some of the designs that we see in nature; for example, the arrangement of sunflower seeds. This mathematical formula embodies a ratio of 1 to 1.61 that is

> There are geometrical ratios in a range of natural phenomena. The design of ferns and sunflowers is arranged according to the golden mean and the Fibonacci sequence. This sense of a visual order in nature is appealing to the human eye. We prefer order over chaos in our lives and nature points to an ordering principle in the very fabric of existence.

pleasing to the human eye. It is seen in many ancient structures, like the front of the Pantheon in Rome. If you examine your credit card or an A4 piece of paper, the ratio of the smallest side to the largest is based on the golden ration. It is just a pleasing ratio to the human eye! It is also linked to another mathematical formula known as the Fibonacci sequence. The geometry in the spirals of sunflower seeds or a nautilus shell all increase and spiral according to a mathematical formula discovered by the Italian mathematician Leonardo Bonacci, or Fibonacci, way back in the twelfth century. The repeated mathematical designs, ratios and patterns in nature are pleasing to the human eye because they allow for more fluent visual processing. They mean that the eye can scan over a landscape and process the visual data with a minimum of neural processing effort. So it is easier to look at natural landscapes instead of city landscapes because the latter are full of irregular angles and shapes that have no intrinsic or repeated pattern. Modern city streets are an amalgam of different designs, neon lights and marketing paraphernalia that require more visual processing from the brain, which is demanding and tiring.

Humans have always had a preference for order, ratios and patterns. An ordered universe brings food, safety and shelter. Chaos brings disease, war and pestilence. The ancient architects of Newgrange and Stonehenge aligned their monuments to the predicted movements of the sun, thus establishing that order existed. We were safer in a universe built upon form, geometry and repeated patterns in cosmological orbits. Two Russian scientists, Vladimir Poponin and Peter Gariaev, conducted an experiment where they tracked the movement and layout of photons in a test tube. The photons were distributed in a completely unordered pattern, clinging to the sides of the test tube and clustered at the bottom of the container. Samples of human DNA were then placed in the closed tube with the photons. Remarkably, the photons began to arrange themselves in regular patterns in the presence of living human material. Furthermore, when the DNA was removed the photons held their ordered sequencing, rather than reverting to their previous haphazard arrangements. They concluded that DNA, the stuff we are made of, is an ordering agent indicating that there is, indeed, a preference for order in our biological makeup. This theory is supported by the effect of the fractal patterns and geometrical sequencing in nature on our central nervous system.

Studies show that even natural colours like greens, blues and browns allow us to be more restful and less stressed. This would make sense, as the older parts of our brain are more at home in a natural environment. The greens of fields, meadows and forest canopies also remind the brain of an abundant food supply. Where there is green there is food, security and order. For the older brain, the colours of the great outdoors are a trigger of nutrition and supply, which sates ancient survival mechanisms. Albert Einstein put it thus, 'The most important decision we make is whether we believe we live in a friendly or hostile universe.' When we walk through the forest the lush green shadows on the forest floor are supermarket shelves to more archaic systems that sate, reassure and sooth. Where there is abundance there is order and where there is order there is the sense that we might just live in a friendly universe after all.

Comparative studies have been done in American cities that have compared the behaviour of people who have a view of greenery, along with access to it, with those who don't. The residents who were immersed in the asphalt and greys of urban life showed more characteristics of aggressive behaviour, along with some severe and milder levels of violence. There were higher levels of burglary, homicide, assault and arson according to police reports. The crime levels in areas deprived of greenery were almost doubled. One theory – although there are, of course, many factors at play here – is that residents who had access to green areas socialised in them more frequently with their neighbours. They got to know each other and looked out for the needs of the group, instead of the needs of the individual. Needless to say, they reported less loneliness and they were also more generous when it came to charitable activities.

Our eyes have evolved over millions of years to only see a small sliver of the light spectrum. They find it relatively easy to filter out the light that's not needed, like infrared or ultraviolet. Pythons, on the other hand, can see infrared light and dragonflies can see ultraviolet light. Our eyes are not mere receptors; they have decision-making functions. They make initial choices as to what data makes its way into the thalamus and then onto the visual cortex near the rear of the brain. The eyes play a crucial function in constructing the brain's conception of reality and, as organs, they work really hard during the day. The importance of the role that they perform gives us an insight into how we should care for our eyes.

While our eyes have evolved to easily filter unwanted light from a natural environment, they find it more challenging and energy sapping to filter unwanted artificial light. We spend almost 90 per cent of our time in artificial light, in particular, florescent light, LED and the blue light emitted from electronic screens and devices. Artificial light is high-energy light and, in fact, blue light is designed to keep us awake. It doesn't want us to rest or take a break and is intrinsic to the addictive technologies behind social media platforms. It overstimulates the brain, which is why many of us now have trouble falling to sleep. Compare this to the restful and fluid visual processing in nature, and the benefits of green therapy become more apparent. How much easier it was for monks and our ancient forebears, who rose and slept according to seasonal natural light!

Sounds

There is a line of thought which suggests that the health benefits of nature lie as much in what it is not as what it is. As we have shown, there are many reasons why being amongst trees and greenery is good for us. Another reason why we can benefit from it is because it gives us a break and a reprieve from all the pressures and stimuli of the urban world of concrete grey and walls of glass. In this way, again, nature acts as a threshold, a crossing from one place to the other. Crossing all thresholds involves a separation or passage of some kind. We leave something behind. This is why we like going away on our holidays or going out for a meal to socialise. We leave behind the deadening world of routine for something different. When it comes to our time spent in nature, one threshold we cross involves separating ourselves from the world of everyday noise to the sweeter soundscape of the countryside.

When we examined how nature affects us visually, we noted that the eyes work very hard processing data and so they get tired and worn out. The same applies to the functioning of our ears. They are not merely two openings in our head to allow noise in. Our ears also have to process data and internally change shape to filter out unwanted sounds. What we perceive as reality has already been filtered and processed by our senses or else we would be overcome by a sensory overload. So when you walk into a crowded room, your aural receptors will filter out most of the conversations to leave you with one or two along with a general background murmur and hum. It would be quite impossible to tune into every conversation and it is your ears that have to decide which noises make it through to the auditory cortex.

When you want to have a conversation with one particular person in a crowded room, what the ears filter out is called 'noise'. In general, the world has been becoming a very noisy place and has gotten louder by about 50 per cent every thirty years. Studies continuously show that we prefer the sounds of nature to urban sounds. The lapping of waves by a shore, the wind through leaves or the gurgling of a stream are preferred to mechanical, electrical or other man-made noises. Workers have reported feeling happier and more productive when listening to the sounds of nature while they work than listening to white noise or office noise. More startling studies, however, point to the detrimental effects of urban noises and in particular aviation noise.

Florence Williams, in her book *The Nature Fix*, catalogued the effects of aviation noise on people living close to major airports. The limbic brain, which is part of the older networks, interprets the drone of aircraft noise as scarily similar to the rumblings of a tiger in the forest. Needless to say, the higher brain overrides and corrects this, but not all the time. Studies pointed to a 20 per cent increase in hypertension among men aged forty who lived close to airports in many European cities where noise levels were above 50 decibels. The World Health Organization attributes many thousands of deaths per year to stroke and heart attack caused by too much urban noise. Studies of children who lived near noisy airports showed double the normal levels of the stress hormones epinephrine and norepinephrine. They also pointed to lower levels of reading comprehension and memory along with raised levels of hyperactivity. As Williams points out, sometimes you literally can't hear yourself think.

In order to find out more about how noise affects the brain, Williams allowed herself to be hooked up to the heart-rate monitor, among other machines, at the Pennsylvania State University. She describes herself as being particularly sensitive to noise, especially aircraft noise. She was then subjected to the Trier Social Stress Test, which deliberately stresses participants by making them do maths tests and deliver a public speech, and then measures their cortisol levels to ensure that they are, indeed, in a stressed state. It is important to point out that Williams agreed wholeheartedly to this procedure.

In order to restore normal cortisol levels, Williams was allowed to listen to a fifteen-minute video of nature sounds. During it, her heart rate sank to a healthy baseline, aided by the sounds of nature. Then, unbeknownst to her, the sound of a rumbling truck invaded the nature sounds of the video and her heart rate rose significantly. She concluded that urban noise really was a problem for her. Joshua Smyth, a behavioural health psychologist at the university, advised that she should think of soundscapes as a form of therapy. It is a well-known problem that many people eventually give up on stress-reducing therapies like yoga or mediation but Smyth argues that taking twenty minutes in nature is a viable intervention for acute stress and, remarkably, it is as easy as a walk in the park. Williams was advised to immerse herself in water, wind and birdsong, the ultimate triptych of healing soundscapes.

The Shell House at the Parable Garden is aligned to capture the rays of the rising sun on the winter solstice. Ancient alignments such as these confirmed an ordering principle at work in the universe.

5. Going Underground

We are born with two fears, falling and loud noises. Based on our previous chapter, we might well be wary of many other noises as well. As we go through life we acquire other fears as we are an experience-dependant species and derive much of our aversions from what has happened to us in the past. There is a specific fear of being in the water, aquaphobia. There is a fear of being in the air, acrophobia, but, as of this moment, there is no catalogued fear of being on the ground. Instead, being on the ground is where we feel safest and, as a result, there is much talk about the benefits of 'being grounded' when it comes to our general well-being. We will return to this theme later on but, for the moment, we are going to examine our relationship with soil, clay and the earth itself. Here too we will allow our senses to be our navigation tools.

Standing on the ground, even the concrete of our neighbourhood, is in itself a very safe experience. We can have a rational fear of being in water. It can also take a while to find our land legs or sense of balance after being on a boat. It is a great feeling when we set our feet on solid ground. In comparison to the unpredictability of life at sea, terra firma is a safe place. Similarly, for those of us who don't like flying, touching down can give us a great sense of reassurance and security. There is no place like home and there is nothing like the feel of firm ground underneath our feet. When we think of the benefits of nature on our health and well-being, the focus oftentimes and understandably remains above ground, at the level of our sight and hearing, but it is into the subterraneous world of roots, soil, seeds and fungi that we will now venture.

Wood Wide Web

The pace and demands of living and working in a modern Western society can drain and deplete us of our vitality and energy. If we feel that the cityscape and office towers have depleted us somewhat, we immediately feel that something different is going on when we venture into the world of a shady, dense and undisturbed woodland. We can feel an immediate sense of peace and tranquillity once we are enveloped by the canopy of overhanging branches in our favourite woodlands. We have examined how the sights and sounds of nature benefit us but there is something absolutely amazing happening on the forest floor where decay and darkness give way to a miraculous world of life and light. If everything in our world celebrates speed, everything in the forest celebrates slowness. If everything in our world celebrates life at all cost, everything on the forest floor celebrates the miracle of death.

It can take some trees up to seven hundred years to reach old age and in their entire lifetime, they may only propagate one or two new saplings. Sapling children grow extremely slowly in the shade of their parent trees. This slow pace creates stronger root systems and more resilient trunks and barks. Slow growth in the forest is strong growth. A sapling tree might grow in the shade of its parent for up to seventy years, strengthening and rooting. It is only with the death of the parent trees that the opportunity for vigorous new life really arrives. When the old tree dies, an aperture of new light opens up in the canopy, and the sapling can begin to grow at an unprecedented rate, extending leaf and branch into the halo of sunlight that has just opened above. Until they die, the parent tree has ensured slower growth, greater resilience and longevity for the new sapling.

Yet it is really when the old tree crashes to the forest floor that the true miracle of life begins. Mature trees can support up to two thousand insects and creatures from more than two hundred species in their canopies. A dead tree, however, actually supports more life. Remarkably, up to a fifth of all animal and plant life depends on dead wood lying on the forest floor. This is why in properly managed woodlands dead trees are no longer removed. Instead, they are allowed to decompose and rot, so as to seed and incubate the next generation of woodland life. Young spruce often begin their lives in the rotting timbers of their parents in a process that is known as cadaver rejuvenation. In the world of humans, death is the end. In the shady world of the woodlands, death is just the beginning.

It is partly in the subversion of our world that the forest floor takes on its awe and allure. It was Peter Wohlleben in his celebrated *The Hidden Life of Trees* who contributed greatly to our current understanding of what is going on underneath the forest floor. He is a forester in Germany and his fascinating story begins with an observation he made about an old dead beech trunk. Based on the level of internal rot and humus, he guessed the tree had been chopped down maybe five hundred years previously. Yet somehow the stump, this ancient remnant, was still very much alive. Fascinated, he stood and stared at the remains of the living dead tree. The gnarled remains of the tree looked like a concentric circle of old stones but they were alive with green chlorophyll.

By definition, dead things don't live, so Wohlleben figured that it must be the neighbouring beech trees that were somehow keeping the wooden sarcophagus alive. This was only possible either through their root system or remotely through fungal networks. Scientists have discovered that trees of the same species remain connected subterraneously through their root system. It is sometimes referred to as the 'wood wide web'. Through this network, they exchange nutrients and, in times of need, help out their neighbours. According to Darwin, the tips of tree roots are like their brains.

Protection from the elements comes from the entire woodland standing strong, so if one tree gets damaged or diseased, the forest itself is weakened. So, no single tree acts alone; instead, when we walk on the forest floor, we are walking on top of a vast, interconnected superorganism. Trees have evolved into social beings because acting alone they cannot control things like climate, but together they can

> The wood wide web of fungal networks and interlocking root systems points to a community under our feet that is based on the strength of the whole as opposed to the independence of the individual. Like trees, humans also thrive with the support and nourishment provided by family, friends and community.

create mini ecosystems, which favours their survival. Together they can control things like temperature, water supply and defence. In established, undisturbed forests, trees can share 'friendships' and have been known to die together, so joined and interdependent have they become through their root system.

Yet why would a group of beech trees keep alive a five-hundred-year-old great-great-grandparent? Why didn't the beech trees keep alive all their old ancestors? Unless we can learn to speak directly to the trees, it would appear that questions such as these will remain unanswered, which makes them the best types of questions. Walking through woods and observing incredulous phenomena such as these only further instils in us the sense that we really have crossed over into the different world. It is awe in the presence of nature that takes us out of ourselves and beyond the small world of our everyday routines into something vast, connected and mysterious. Unanswered questions dazzle our neural pathways into new and refreshing ways of thinking. This is the very definition of awe and wonder as we are stirred into insight and intrigue by the mysterious and the miraculous on a simple forest floor. There is no tonic like a fresh way of thinking, and the riddles of a primeval forest will keep us guessing about the memory and friendships of trees long after we've crossed back into our world. We want to lose some old thing at the crossing into the woods and perhaps find some new thing to replace it. This is what draws us into the forested realm of root and rot, shadow and shade. In the words of Scottish-American naturalist John Muir, 'And into the forest I go, to lose my mind and find my soul.'

Fungi and Bacteria

We are aware of the need to save the planet but really, as we have seen, it is the planet that is trying to save us. We have failed to come to grips with how we are supposed to live on earth and, as a result, we have warmed it too much through our over-reliance on fossil fuels. We have taken carbon from the ground and deposited it in the atmosphere, leading to global warming. This directly affects the health of our oceans, ice caps and land masses. Yet deep down under our feet, in the wood wide web, there are processes going on that are attempting to reverse the effects of our carbon footprint. It is called soil sequestration and, thankfully, the ground beneath us is the biggest terrestrial carbon sink on the planet.

Trees remove carbon molecules from the atmosphere and transform them into carbon sugars. These are then fed to various fungi and bacteria that gather around the root tips waiting for their sugary treats. Trees communicate on the wood wide web using the fungal networks that extend just under the forest floor. Trees donate nutrients and communicate with damaged or diseased trees through the fungal hyphae that connect different root systems. If a tree needs a particular mineral, the fungal mycelia, or network of hyphae, will source it and return it to the root tips. In return for this favour, the fungi get carbon sugars from the trees. Once the carbon sugars are digested, larger predator protozoa and nematodes digest the bacteria and fungi themselves. The carbon gets stored in the bodies of their predators and remains safely underground. In return for their dinner, the predators excrete plentiful amounts of precious minerals, which are fed back to the trees through the root system. It is a perfect barter system in which the microorganisms of the soil get carbon and the sugar daddies get minerals – and through which we might just get saved.

In this way, carbon gets removed from the atmosphere and ends up stored in the multitude of networks of microorganisms living in the root system of our forests and woodlands. This is why trees play such an important role in reversing the effects of climate change. A single hardwood tree can sequester up to a ton of carbon in forty years. That's a lot of carbon. It is estimated that over two million tonnes of carbon is stored in the trees in the city of London alone. The incredible partnership between roots and microorganisms is well documented in Kristin Ohlson's aptly titled book *The Soil Will Save Us;* however, the story of soil bacteria and green therapy doesn't end there.

Soil Health

In the context of the current ecological challenges facing humanity, a new language is emerging around soil health. If a soil is healthy, it is teeming with these organic networks, which are not only good for carbon sequestration but also help to remove pollutants from water supplies caused by intensive agricultural practices. These microorganisms help the soil to retain water and its structure, thus preventing soil erosion, an issue that can result in the loss of swaths of fertile land with up to seventy-five billion tonnes of soil eroded each year. Fungal spores are even known to be able to cleanse polluted soil from waste or spilled petroleum. Fungal mycelia can actually eat petrol! Bacteria that are found in the ground are not just good for soil health, however; they are also good for our health.

Medical research has developed a 'hygiene hypothesis', which posits that children today have less exposure to microorganisms than previous generations, possibly due to less playtime outdoors in nature. They're missing out on the healthy way of being dirty in the great outdoors. This in turn has weakened their immune system. One focus of research is on a bacterium called Mycobacterium vaccae or M. vaccae for short. This bacterium is now found in ordinary garden soil but was first discovered in Uganda by an immunologist called John Stanford. He noticed that people who lived near Lake Kyoga had a better response to particular leprosy vaccines. After further research, he attributed the increased efficacy of the vaccine to those who were exposed to M. vaccae, which was found in the nearby soil.

The term 'microbiome' refers to the culture of bacteria that lives in our gut or digestive tract. It's our personal colony of microbes. In the last twenty years or so research on the link between the quality of our microbiome and our general health has gained real intensity. Researchers believe that bacteria such as M. vaccae can be ingested or breathed in when we get dirt on our hands and become part of our gut culture. Somehow this can have a positive effect not only on our immune system but also on our general mental health. M. vaccae has also been linked to increased levels of serotonin in the prefrontal cortex of the brain, which raises our levels of happiness.

Research into the exact nature of the relationship between bacteria and our immune systems and emotional states is still at an early stage but, as Dr Li says in his book *Shinrin-yoku: The Art and Science of Forest-Bathing*, 'Every time you dig in your garden or eat a vegetable plucked from the ground, you will be ingesting M. vaccae and giving yourself this boost.' So the general advice is to get out in the garden, take off the gardening gloves and get yourself as mucky as you can. It is the healthy way of being dirty. A single teaspoon of good garden soil can contain up to a billion soil microbes. Professor Graham Rook of the University of London developed the 'hygiene hypothesis' and called it the 'old friends hypothesis'. He argues that we should not think of ourselves as individuals, but instead as ecosystems with microbial partners. Many of these microbes live in the soil, on plants, on leaves and in the general natural environment. We have coexisted with them in a healthy partnership for millions of years. Every time we lie down on the forest floor, hold the bark of a tree or plant a flower, we are immersing ourselves into an ancient relationship every bit as generous and productive as the networks inside the wood wide web.

6. Healthy Scents

There is something instinctive and natural about taking in deep breaths when we are out in nature. Partly, our relax and respond nervous system kicks in, which allows us to de-stress and take deep breaths down into the pits of our stomach. There's nothing like the smell of fresh air but in this chapter we're going to delve into the exact make-up of forest air and find out why it is so good for us. Some people love the smell of the earth just after rain, and there happens to be a very good reason for this. It all goes back to that ancestral part of our brain that survived out in the open for millions of years.

Our oldest sources of anxiety were centred around famine, drought and predators. These fears are still embedded deep in our neural networks, so whenever we assuage these sources of anxiety and worry, we naturally feel better. We can imagine the dread of our forebears when drought struck. Nervously they would have watched their animals and kin languish and wilt. As a species, however, we are born survivors and we can attribute this to our very keen sense of smell. We haven't developed the ability to smell water but we have evolved to be able to detect the damp smell of earth after it has rained. Bacteria in the soil, such as M. vaccae, gives off a particular smell when it is moist. It's called geosmin. It is basically the smell of the ground after it has rained. We can also smell it off root vegetables, cheeses and some wines. Our ancestors may not have seen the rain coming or falling if it was during the night, but the next morning they could detect if geosmin was in the air. If it was, it meant that there was some water close by and they just had to follow their noses. The ability to smell geosmin enabled our ancestors to survive drought. Research shows that we can detect this particular smell in levels as low as five parts to a trillion. It is the smell of survival.

There is another smell mixed in with geosmin after it rains, and it is the smell that comes off of wet rocks. Plants survive long spells of drought by storing precious oils in the soil and rocks around their roots. When it rains the fresh water releases these oils and that creates a particular smell called petrichor, which can be translated as 'essence of stone'. So the fragrances of bacteria, soil and rocks that fill the air after a long dry spell are particularly favourable to our species. We might have water on tap, but parts of our brain still like to be able to open our innate survivor's manual to know where the closest supply of water is located. Our primal link to these wet smells is so strong that it is now being artificially added to some perfumes and fragrances.

Forest Air

Whereas other senses rely on the nervous system to send signals to the brain, the olfactory system has direct access. Our survival depends on being able to respond to scents immediately as they can be the forewarnings of danger. Molecules from various fragrances and odours pass directly from our nasal cavity right into the primal areas of our brain. These are then processed by the amygdala to assess if a fight or flight response is needed. The amygdala is wired directly to the hippocampus, which stores a range of our memories. This system quickly matches smells to past experiences to see if an immediate response is needed. The smell of smoke is an obvious example of this emergency response. Unfortunately, we are wired to worry, which is why assuring our brains with the more pleasant scents of survival is so important for our own self-regulation.

The smell of black earth in dark dripping forests after rain is a wonderfully sensual experience. Yet within this fragrance hides even

> The air in the conifer forest and the pine scents are not only refreshing and mood enhancing, they also contain immune-boosting compounds and molecules that can strengthen our immune system and help to fight cancer.

more surprises for enthusiasts of green therapy. Swirling in the air are unseen pharmacies laden with free prescriptions for one of the most important defence mechanisms in the human body – the immune system. As the world experienced the Covid-19 global pandemic, immunity against the virus was at the forefront of everyone's thoughts. Restrictions were put on people's movement and many tried to get into forests and parks if they were within their parameters. The lucky ones made it into forests because one of the most immune-boosting activities we can do is go for a walk in the woods.

When we examined the dynamics of the wood wide web, we discovered that trees can communicate and support each other through their root systems and accompanying benevolent fungal networks. Trees also communicate with each other through special molecules that are released into the air called phytoncides. Phytoncides and terpenes are organic hydrocarbons that are found in the essential oils of plants. Plants deliberately emit these compounds if diseases or pests attack them. The neighbouring trees or plants then begin to create antibodies and defences to repel the pests. Remember, in the forest, trees protect each other from predators and the elements because it is easier for a tree to survive in a forest than alone out in open spaces.

The alarm system not only alerts other trees, but it can also attract particular predators to kill the pests. When we walk in the forest and breathe in the aroma of all those essential oils we are really immersing ourselves in the forest's own immune and emergency response system. The phytoncides can attract particular insects to come and attack the pests annoying the trees. Phytoncides can also attack pollutants near trees and so they can also act as an air filtration system. This is why the air in a forest seems clearer and cleaner. Remarkable research is now emerging which suggests that the immune system of the trees in the forest has a beneficial effect on the human immune system.

The Immune System

Killer T cells are special white blood cells that patrol our circulatory system. If they find a cell that has been invaded by a virus, they proceed to kill that cell. It is the exact same as an assassination hit. This group of assassins also targets tumour cells or cells that could turn cancerous. The research that has emerged, however, shows that the amount of Killer T cells in these roving hit squads increases after we have spent time in the forest. Doctor Li conducted a study with a group of participants in the Iiyama forest region. After three days and two nights in the forest, the amount of natural killer cells increased by 50 per cent. Killer T cells also become more active by 50 per cent when we are immersed in the forest. Remarkably, he discovered that this level of activity lasted for a further thirty days. Yet a question remained. We know that reduced levels of stress boost our immune system, so was it possible that the increase in Killer T cells was simply due to the calming effects of forest bathing? In order to find out, Dr Li locked willing participants into hotel rooms for three nights. In some rooms he placed humidifiers to vaporise oil from hinoki cypress trees. The other participants enjoyed natural hotel scented aromas. The results showed that participants in the hinoki-scented rooms had a 20 per cent increase in the specialised cells.

The science behind green therapy is still at an early stage and remains inconclusive and, therefore, time spent in nature should in no way replace conventional medical treatments. The reader will be unable to count how many more immune cells are active in the bloodstream after forest bathing but one thing they will be able to do is assess their mood and sense of vitality. We might not be able to apply rigorous scientific methods to our time spent in nature but we will know if the mind, the body or the emotions feel different. We are time bound by scientific research and quite possibly in years to come more and more research will point to even more surprising data and insights.

Ancient Stories

When Peter Wohlleben takes visitors through the ancient deciduous forests that he manages, they report that their heart feels lighter and that they feel like they are 'right at home'. Why is it so? We know that the older parts of our brain lived in those forests for many millions of years but why is it that our immune systems are so mysteriously linked? Ultimately, it is up to each individual to answer that for themselves because that relationship will be as unique as every person ever born. One way that humans ask the big questions and also attempt to answer them is through our mythologies. We create myths to try to understand ourselves and our place on this earth. Myths embrace mysteries; they never really attempt to solve them because that would destroy the power embedded in the primal act of questioning in the first place. We created gods to help us explain the vagaries of our existence, from storms and famines to feasts and harvests. The Judaeo-Christian mythology in Genesis presents a single God, who created everything and provided *Adamah*, or 'red earth', the soil to till and care for. It was intended to be an act of never-ending stewardship. He who was created from the soil was placed back on it to work, grow and prosper.

In her book *Braiding Sweetgrass*, Robin Kimmerer draws upon the myth of the Skywoman in order to explore our relationship with the green earth. The Skywoman descended into our world through a column of light that formed from a hole in the Skyworld. There was only dark water below her, but the geese spread their wings to save her descent from the formless void below. The aquatic animals knew she needed a solid ground to stand upon, so the turtle offered her his back, which she gratefully accepted. Then a muskrat descended into the deeps to create some ground for her to stand upon. He retrieved some mud and placed it upon the turtle. In gratitude, she began a dance of thanksgiving but the small piece of mud grew and grew until the whole earth was covered. In her hand she clutched some seeds and plants from the Skyworld and these she scattered onto the ground until it turned brown and green with fertile life. Earth as we know it had been formed.

In Native understanding, it is the plants and trees that came first. They pre-exist the human species and the later human arrivals are regarded as youngsters, the younger brothers of Creation. The plants have more experience of growing, sharing and surviving and it is to them that we must look for example. The plants are our teachers and they teach us by the example that they give. They teach us about the cycles of the seasons, how to sow and how to grow. They teach us about the health of the soil and how to reap and harvest. Most of all, though, they teach us how to be human. It is to these lessons that we turn in part three.

Practical Tips

1. Boosting Immunity and Anticancer Defences

According to Dr Li's research, a day in the woods can boost the levels of Killer T cells by 40 per cent. Two days raises levels by 50 per cent. The activity of the cells is also increased by 50 per cent for another thirty days. In order to receive this boost to our immunity all we have to do is breathe in the phytoncides, so it's really rather simple.

- For best results spend as much time in the forest as you can. Terpenes and phytoncides are also most plentiful and active after rain so this is a good time to enter the woods.
- Even though all plants release phytochemicals, trees release the most powerful anticancer terpenes. Conifers release the most terpenes, in particular pine, spruce, fir, cedar and cypress. After that, the best deciduous trees are beech, oak, birch and hazel.
- If you can plant blueberries, raspberries, apple trees and tomatoes in your garden, these are also a very good source of antioxidants. Antioxidants capture free radicals in the body, thus preventing cancers. An anticancer garden could also include onions, leeks, broccoli, kale and cabbage.
- Try to forest bathe once a month for a boost in your immunity and defences against cancer. The summer months are very suitable as phytoncides are most concentrated during warmer weather.

2. Sight

Natural light is known to raise our levels of serotonin and vitamin D so getting out in the sunlight is always good for us. Serotonin makes us feel happier, calmer and more serene while suppressing feelings of worry or anxiety. Many who are diagnosed with depression also have lower serotonin levels, though this may not be the only cause for depression.

- Human psychology favours order over chaos. Chaos summons up feelings of threat and danger. Order summons up feelings of safety. The fractal patterns that can be found in nature calm the mind and help us to feel that we live in a safe and ordered world. Search for fractal patterns in ferns, trees and sunflowers. Anywhere where there are repeated patterns is soothing for the human mind. You will find them in the most surprising of places!

- To get the best benefits from the sights of nature we need to spend a bit of time really allowing ourselves to look. Nature operates very slowly so we have to give it time. If we stay still in a natural environment, foxes, otters, birds and all sorts of creatures will make themselves known. The key is to be still and silent and really examine your environs.

- Our eyes get very tired but will be soothed by the colours of nature. Research shows that green and sky blue is a particularly pleasant combination so sunny days are especially beneficial.

- After a while it is good to close our eyes to let them have a rest. It is very soothing to place both of your hands over your eyes as an extra layer of protection and rest. Small moments of self-care like these in nature enhance the benefits for the body.

3. Sound

When new runways are opened at international airports, there can often be a reported increase in strokes and cardiovascular issues. Research showed that people who slept under the flight paths were releasing stress chemicals throughout the night as the amygdala was interpreting the sounds of the aircraft as similar to ancient predators. The sounds of nature, on the other hand, stimulate the parasympathetic nervous system into action.

- The brain prefers nature sounds to man-made or mechanical sounds. So when you go out into nature for some green therapy, it's best to go to places that are free from traffic, aviation or agricultural noise.
- The sounds of nature that we most like are water, wind and birdsong so pick the times when birdsong is at its loudest in your environment.
- When we go into nature and try to listen to its sounds it can be more difficult than appreciating its sights. Often when the external noise is lowered the internal noise of our thoughts is raised, which can be distracting. The practical tips at the end of part one can be helpful here. Utilise the practice of thresholds, slow down your movements and try to find a quiet shelter to sit in. Allow your breathing to soften and become more at ease.
- You can start by listening to the nearest sounds first and trying to identify them. This focuses the mind that might want to wander. Then see if you can detect the sounds furthest away from you, the wind through trees or waves on a nearby shore. Is there birdsong or any water sounds? Again, all we have to do is be still. The sounds will stimulate our relax and respond systems. We just have to let it happen.
- Eventually you might feel comfortable enough to close your eyes to enhance your hearing. Like the eyes, the ears get tired so if you want you can gently cup your hands over your ears to help rest and restore them. As general rule, try to avoid human sounds when renewing yourself in nature. Most of the demands in our lives come from other humans.

4. Smell

As we've noted, forest smells boost our immunity but they also lift our moods. When we walk in woodlands we are smelling the natural compounds in essential and aromatherapy oils that we can buy in shops. The smell of these oils can lift depression and lower anxiety.

- The smells of the oils are in the air of the forest so once we are immersed in woodland we cannot avoid the smells. Conifers emit the strongest smells and if you find sap on the sides of trees, you will smell the essential oils right there on the bark.
- Phytoncides can be beneficial for depression and anxiety but they can also help to lower blood pressure and increase heart rate variability (a marker for activity in the parasympathetic nervous system) because they suppress sympathetic nervous activity.
- Phytoncides can be found on bushes, fruit trees and most plants. It is good to physically touch greenery to get the smells and oils onto your hands. Physically touching greenery can raise the concentration of phytoncides in the air around you. It is also useful for retraining motor and sensory skills if needed.
- The scent of rose oil or roses can have a particularly pleasant effect on us. Rose blossoms contain a substance called indole. Indole is also found in amniotic fluid in our mother's womb so this might be one reason why we associate roses with love, warmth and comfort.
- After rain, the scents of geosmin and petrichor are also in the air. They have a calming effect on the more ancient parts of our brain as they indicate the presence of water.
- The smell and feel of good soil on our hands contains the bacterium M. vaccae, which helps to boost our mood and our immune system. It is always good to get our hands dirty during green therapy and this has even more benefits after rain.

PART 3
Encounter

this is the recipe of life
said my mother
as she held me in her arms as i wept
think of those flowers you plant
in the garden each year
they will teach you
that people too
must wilt
fall
root
rise
in order to bloom

Rupi Kaur, The Sun and Her Flowers

7. Patterns

After Skywoman stood upon the earth for the first time, it began to be populated with more life. Green sprouted everywhere, the fresh ground was fertilised by the seeds she had clenched in her hand after her descent. After the greening of the earth, the Creator then made the Original Man and, though he was the First Man, he was the last to be created. He was fashioned from four sacred elements and given the name Nanabozho. Before his time, the plants and animals learned how to live upon this new earth and gathered wisdom and knowledge that could later be passed onto him. These green guardians tested the foods growing upon the earth to see which were poisonous and which were edible. The animals learned how to build shelters and how to hunt and gather. They learned how to read the signs and omens of weather, woven as they were into the winds and sounds and slants of light. The Creator placed Nanabozho upon the earth and explained that his first task was not to learn how to control the world, but to learn from it how to be human.

His first teachers were the birds, beavers, spiders and beetles. He learned how to make hooks from the burdock thistle and learned how to dive from the kingfisher. He fashioned nets to catch fish after he watched a spider weave silken webs. He learned how to collect water from the beetles and lizards and how to store food from the squirrel. The corncrakes tutored him in resilience and the sparrows, gold finches and blue jays taught him about parenting and fidelity. When he tracked wolves he observed leadership and loyalty. They also taught him how to rest and to only take enough food as was needed. The foxes in the forests were highly protective and adaptive. He watched and learned. His early work ethic and engineering skills were forged along the banks of still rivers where beavers were flexing early architectural skills. Soon the First Man became many and he watched meerkats resolve conflict and flamingos form friendships. The African wild dogs embraced primitive voting systems and hermit crabs used networking to find suitable housing. And all the time he watched and he observed, as his elderly brethren of mole and meerkat mentored and instructed him as to how to live sustainably and respectfully on the earth that had fallen from the sky.

There now exist entire industries and technologies that base their research and innovation on biomimicry. Often engineering designs are based on organic blueprints. New social policies and schemes now owe their efficiency to biological strategies and during the Covid-19 pandemic it was initially to the super immune systems of bats that researchers first turned their attention. The virus infected us; the bats just carried it. Nature displays incredible methods of fighting off pathogens and, as we've seen, fields and forests provide amazing resilience and adaptability to predators and airborne threats. Fractal patterns in leaves and golden ratios embedded in sunflowers always pointed to an intelligence hidden in the natural landscape. This is why, for example, the latest and most efficient wind turbine design mimics the aerodynamics of a diving kingfisher and the air patterns surrounding a falling maple seed.

Recalibrating Our Relationship

So from Native ancient mythologies to contemporary engineering and biomedical research, there is a slow but evolving inversion of the perceived hierarchical structure of where we position ourselves in the natural habitat. Sometime after the Enlightenment period, humans placed themselves at the top of the food chain and decided the earth and its resources were at its sole disposal for whatever benefit was needed. We have somehow always decided that we can own and control various parts of the earth. It might only be a half acre site or a terraced garden but it was our perception that we knew best what to do with this patch of green. Agricultural practices on fields and farmsteads mirrored what was going on in gardens everywhere; it was the human who controlled and determined the agenda of what would grow, even though every piece of the earth has its own organic blueprint and intention. These codes are written along root systems, the treads of fungal filaments and deposits of native seedlings.

In order to become a student of the planet, we have to cease being its master. Mary Reynolds is an Irish garden and landscape designer and the youngest woman ever to win the gold medal at the Chelsea Flower Show. In her book *The Garden Awakening*, she documents how she re-evaluated her relationship with the earth when she realised that she wasn't working in harmony with the land in her garden designs. The land in her designed gardens did not want to remain the way she had planned. Nature has its own plans and designs for what needs to grow in a given aspect, a given landscape and a given soil. Nature has its own intention yet often our garden maintenance and agricultural practices struggle against this. Our love of lawns is a typical example of how we determine what happens to the piece of earth in our care. Reynolds has created a movement called We Are The Ark. She is inviting anyone who owns a piece of land to give some portion of it back to nature to let nature grow what it wants to grow.

We don't like messiness in our gardens in the same way that we don't like messiness in our lives, but she points out that there is more life in a messy piece of wilderness than on a manicured lawn. What is wild is alive. The creatures of the earth can't live on open lawns but they can find safety and security in long grasses and bushes and little bug hotels. We need to let old bits of wood die and rot in our gardens. We need to leave clumps of twigs and branches in little stacks so that beetles and bugs can create a home. We like things to be clean and tidy but nature

This Ark protects two acres of wilderness composed of woodland and marsh. It is an untouched habitat that is home to many animals, birds and wildflowers.

needs organic homes untouched by humans. In the same way that we need a hygienic way to be dirty, we also need an orderly way to be messy.

As life returns to these patches of wilderness, biodiversity is given a chance to strengthen at this time of ecological crisis. Eventually, given time, a piece of wilderness untouched by humans will support trees and even greater levels of carbon sequestering. We are in the middle of a global ecological crisis but if we could leave the earth alone, she actually knows what to do to heal herself. Our food chain needs biodiversity and we need millions more trees to act as carbon sinks. If we can stop and listen and do nothing but observe, the earth is teaching us and telling us what to do. Now more than ever, we need to become more like Nanabozho and become the students of these green elders and teachers.

Different Rhythms

As we begin to recalibrate our relationship with nature, we can begin to learn how to live in a more meaningful and ecologically sustainable fashion. Yet her lessons go far deeper that environmental stewardship. Nature can also teach us how to be human and just as the earth is trying to teach us how to heal her own land, she can also teach us how to heal ourselves. Technology promised us so much but in reality gave us so little. Many of us are feeling depleted by the pace and pressures of a Western lifestyle, yet we can also learn how to do acts of restorative kindness to ourselves. How we treat the land can be viewed as a mirror of how we treat ourselves. If we have been seen to overwork the land to the point where its soils are eroded and precious minerals depleted, many of us have also overworked ourselves to the point of stress and endless fatigue.

Nature doesn't ask us to do more. Nature asks us to do less. The wisdom in acts of restorative kindness is to let go of our need to control and just let nature be. Just as we need to rewild our gardens, we also need to rewild ourselves. Again, how we treat nature is how we treat ourselves. To rewild a human being is to simply allow them to be at one with the natural rhythms that we witness in the natural world around us. It is not to do nothing because nature does quite a lot, but it is to do everything at a different pace and tempo.

In old-growth forests trees grow slowly but then live for hundreds of years. It takes hundreds of years for an oak to reach maturity but then it can live on for four to five hundred years. There is a lot for us to learn from these old-growth forests and when we are in them we can do more for ourselves beyond the natural boost to our immune systems. Trees, like us, are living organic systems and we can observe and learn how to mimic some of their dynamics, especially when it comes to resilience and longevity. Old-growth forests know how to thrive and it all comes down to timing, natural rhythms and pace. It all comes down to simply slowing down.

Rest and Slowing Down

Pioneering trees are the first to take hold in a piece of new forest. Trees like birches are the first to sprout and grow. They grow fast and reproduce new cells speedily. They shoot up, displaying their branches and finery quickly as they take their foothold in the virgin soil. But this new growth, at such a speed, comes at a price. The cells grow quickly but are filled with air and are, therefore, more susceptible to predators and disease. These adolescent trees typically burn themselves out with premature development and their crowns are sparse and porous. This is good news for the competitors slowly emerging from the forest floor below. Baby oaks and maples will take their time, but due to the birch's sparse crown precious light is filtering down to these new contenders. They enjoy the shade and protection of these taller trees, yet by the time they reach the same height as the birches, they have burned themselves out and are beginning to wilt and die. So the first lesson from the forest is that slow and steady wins the race.

In part, this is what forests do to us; they slows us down and teach us the importance of rest. Many city dwellers try to grow forest trees indoors or on windowsills but it just doesn't work. Shorn of their natural habitat, the old-growth trees are forced to grow too quickly because there is constant warmth and light, which are the catalysts for growth. Trees need a winter to rest and hibernate. This cycle of growth and rest is the one that protects them long into old age. Trees need to become completely inactive during winter or else they can be severely damaged. If there is moisture in the trunk during heavy frosts, the timber can expand and the tree can literally burst open. Moisture comes with activity but when the tree shuts down all its systems in early autumn, moisture levels decrease dramatically; therefore, there is no water to freeze during harsh and freezing winters. The sap will rise again in springtime, in tune with warmer winds and rising temperatures.

Survival, resilience and longevity all come with winter's rest and this wintering in lasts for a long time. Leaves begin to fall in early autumn and signs of new life don't appear until late spring so there are many months of shutting down and completely resting from all activity. The current pandemic of stress, which the World Health Organization has called the greatest threat to our health, is caused by too much activity and too little rest. We are living creatures like the trees and we need to learn this crucial lesson from them. We need to learn how to rest; yet, it is a concept that is rarely taught to us. In school, success comes with hard work, and often the advice given to students who are underperforming is to work harder.

Rarely does a report card prescribe that a student needs to rest. Leading entrepreneurs constantly preach that success comes from working harder than your competitors. This is surely true but the cost is a stressful lifestyle that is incredibly damaging to all of the systems in the human body. Ideas can act like harmful viruses and the current and incessant drive to work, perform and produce operates completely contrary to how living organisms live and thrive. Living things need to rest and restore but too often our species has embraced competition and control.

We need to learn how to rest to help the sympathetic nervous system that is becoming all too active in the modern workplace. This fight or flight response damages our immune, digestive and cardiovascular systems to name but a few. The balm of the parasympathetic nervous system is needed to repair and restore our minds and bodies to health, but contemporary lifestyles make it difficult for the body to kick-start this response. We fill our downtime with screen time, which is a known stressor, when in reality we need to use our downtime to completely rest. This is not just the lesson of the forest. Trees can also actually help us to rest as is demonstrated by the research that comes from forest bathing.

Rest means doing nothing. It is not the same as relaxation or even sleep. The body is very active during sleep, and does not completely rest, which is why we can often wake up quite tired. So if we don't get rest during sleep we have to consciously allow our bodies and minds to rest during the day. Resting systems is something that we need to do while we are awake and we can do it in many different ways. Nature

| Seat by stone wall in the Parable Garden.

itself, free from the demands of work, others and social media is a perfect prescription. This is one of the ways that nature is good for us because it provides a break from all the demands that a home or office can place upon us. Rewilding our gardens means that we don't have to work all the time in them. They can become natural habitats for just sitting and staring and doing nothing.

Wilderness

The wilderness is one of the most beneficial landscapes to visit. By definition it is untouched by humans and, therefore, invites no thoughts of work, duty or control. These ecosystems have been left alone and they have been allowed to simply be. This is the lesson for us from the wilderness: to be left alone, to just be. If we can allow a piece of land to just do what it wants to do, we are promoting a dynamic that is completely therapeutic for ourselves. There are no demands placed on a piece of wilderness. It does not have to look pretty and it does not have to produce anything. It can be messy and it can even be ugly. The wonderfully healing insight is that it is allowed to grow exactly the way it wants to, freed from human judgement or interference. When a variety of landscapes were assessed for their different therapeutic benefits, wilderness areas scored highest because of the diversity and variety of plant and animal life. Areas like lawns with the highest levels of human control scored the least because of their banality and uniformity.

The human body and mind need this too. Stress comes from the tension that is created when too much weight is placed on a structure. Human stress is caused when too many demands are placed upon us. Absolutely no demands are placed on a piece of wilderness, which makes it the archetypal landscape for human renewal and restoration. It inspired Gerard Manley Hopkins's famous lines, 'O let them be left, wildness and wet; Long live the weeds and the wilderness yet.' When humans are allowed to rest, they don't have to look any particular way and they don't have to act in any particular way. The human who is resting is one that is completely free from the demands of others. This is why we like it, even if we don't manage to get much of it.

The contradiction in our contemporary narrative of endless activity, stimulation and work is that ultimately it is counterproductive. Stressed out human beings eventually reach burnout and, thus, become unproductive. We are like the trees that are gown indoors. If we are overstimulated by ceaseless demands for productivity, something eventually breaks down. We then become increasingly unproductive. Worse still, our ill health becomes a burden to the health system and our caregivers who have to start minding us. It is a central maxim of all self-care programmes that self-care is not selfish. Resting ourselves means that we are taking responsibility for our own health. It means that someone else won't have to eventually take care of us. Self-care is not selfish; it is selfless.

Nature is one of the most productive entities that we know of. It provides our food and sequesters our carbon. It regulates weather patterns and provides food and shelter for ecosystems that provide vital biodiversity. It does all of this only because it takes annual leave from early autumn until late spring. Nature spends over half its time doing absolutely nothing. It just rests but this break is the foundation of a fruitful harvest and immense productivity. All organic systems produce and thrive because they incorporate a natural balance of rest and activity into their operations. It is a seasonal balance of wintering to be followed by summertime harvest and it is one that works perfectly. It is a beautiful balance of bleakness and blossom, scarcity and abundance and is captured wonderfully by the biblical poet who writes, 'To every thing there is a season, and a time to every purpose under the heaven: A time to be born, and a time to die; a time to plant, and a time to pluck up that which is planted' (Ecclesiastes 3:1-2).

We are allowed to rest when we have done enough and our day's work is done. When we immerse ourselves in nature it gives us permission to rest and assures us that we have done enough. It has its own intention of what it wants to do, and is well capable of doing it, so it demands nothing from us. Nature invites us to do nothing so that she can go about her business of cleaning the air and providing cover for the multitude of creatures that call her home. The world tells us constantly that we are not enough and that we need to buy more, do more and look better. Nature invites us into a different space, where we only have to do the small things, like looking and listening and wondering. And, in doing this, she bequeaths to us the lesson that we are enough, just the way we are, and that nothing more is needed. Nature offers us the wild untouched spaces as a metaphor for how we can view ourselves. She offers us the wildness and the weeds and the wilderness as a metaphor for our own self-understanding and as a dispensation from the need to be anything more than we already are.

The essence of the wilderness and the wild places is that they are to remain untouched. These places are allowed to crawl and sprawl with all living things in harmony with none other than nature's own gentle and soft intention to heal the world. In all of this there is a complete absence of judgement because everything is enough and everything is perfect just the way it is. When we look at gardens we are invited into the space of judgement but when we gaze upon the wild places, critique and analysis is temporarily in abeyance. We cannot end the sentence, 'This wild place would be better if …' That's the nature of the wilderness. It cannot be better and it cannot be worse. It just is. To occupy a space free of judgement is anathema to much of our social interactions with other humans. Humans judge themselves and others all the time. In part it stems from that ancient survival part of our brain that fears exclusion from the group, which would inevitably mean death. We are preoccupied by knowing what people think about us, in case we will be excluded. We judge ourselves to make sure we are enough and we judge others as a method of comparing ourselves to the required standards of social acceptance and inclusion.

Safe Space

In the natural world there is no judgement and no comparison. There is no tree better than another tree and on the contrary they prop and support any tree that is struggling in order to protect the whole. This suspension of judgement in nature becomes crucial when we are feeling at our worst because the green place then becomes the safe space. We have an inherent fear of failure because it may lead to our exclusion from the group, but nature just accepts us the way we are. This is why green spaces are becoming more and more useful as spaces for the treatment of mental illness. Many who suffer from stress, depression or anxiety fear the judgement of others in case they are in some way viewed as a failure.

For those who can sit and watch and listen, nature has lessons to teach all year around. When the sap stops rising in autumn, the leaves will start to fall and the ground will be littered with a carpet of amber and auburn, crimson and carmine. The thirteenth-century Persian poet Rumi commented that we too should 'be like a tree and let the dead leaves drop'. In life it is hard to let go of failures, hurt and harsh words but the autumnal shedding points to the necessity of letting go, so as to create a space for growth and new life. Winter envelops the dead leaves and there can be a harsh beauty in a winter landscape given the proper slant of low-lying light. It can also be dreary, bleak and harsh. The ground underfoot can be sodden with decaying leaves, dried only by raw easterly or northerly winds. Nature isn't always beautiful. Much of it can feel banal, abandoned or lacking in vibrancy and luminescence. We live in a world that demands perfection but the natural world weaves puddles, decay and rot into its tapestry of life. In doing so, it invites us to do the same. It invites us to accept the imperfect, to embrace the flawed and seemingly defective parts of ourselves. Despite its appearance, every part of the natural world is vital to maintain its balance and function. Every abandoned ditch and wasteland is home to vital flora and fauna. Even the badlands and barren lands are home and habitat to something alive and thriving. All of nature is not beautiful, but all of nature is vital and indispensable to our biodiversity and the survival of our species. The same applies to us. We are not always beautiful or perfect but our entire life story is intrinsic and essential for our personal growth and development.

Winter wanes and the evenings lengthen to herald springtime. There is something about freshly upturned soil at the beginning of spring that invites the imagination to wonder what might grow. It could be left alone to see what the earth is dreaming for this patch of peaty brown and alluvial sand. Alternatively, we can imagine something that might be harmonious with the intention latent in the ground. We could plant trees, flowers or shrubs or herbs, vegetables or fruit. We just need to look around us to observe what is native. All around at springtime brown stalk is budding into green and the earth is resplendent with the beginnings of new life. The old things have passed and the new things are arriving. Nature mirrors that ancient Taoist teaching that everything is in a state of change and flow, illuminating and unsettling all the stagnant points and places in our lives. Change scares us but everything is changing. The russet carpet of autumn turns to freshly ploughed brown. This is followed by a multitude of green shoots, a host of yellow daffodils and then the gold of harvest. Change scares us but at the same time the stagnation of fear, boredom and loneliness can propel us into a new search for meaning and purpose. Springtime sings an eternal hymn to new life and she proposes the greening of a human soul stuck fast in sadness or despair.

> The wilderness creates a safe space for humans as they are allowed to simply be, without judgement or the demand for perfection. The wilderness invites us to rest, to do nothing, to simply be ourselves.

The gardener's hands dug deep in darkened soil point to the inner work needed to celebrate the fullness of our human existence. Inner work is hard and is rooted in the shadows of dirt and darkness, deep in our core. Yet authentic inner work will be blessed with a summertime harvest as stagnation gives way to flow, death gives way to life and despair gives way to hope. When we immerse ourselves in the cycles of death and life, darkness and light, we are being drawn into the rich dynamics at the heart of authentic living. Life is not easy, but when seeds root and sprout in darkened earth, we see a story being unravelled which goes someway to explaining the deepest yearnings and experience of the human heart. Amidst fractal patterns and birdsong, nature speaks a language of acceptance, compassion and non-judgement. This is a crucial perspective when dealing with our mental health, the topic of our next chapter.

8. Mental Health

If you ever find yourself looking at a mountain or lake scene in a doctor or dentist's waiting room, you might have Roger Ulrich to thank for that. As we noted earlier, his research demonstrated the effects of looking at nature on human physiology. In his research, nature scenes, images and paintings drew out psychological feelings of affection, friendliness and even playfulness. Nature scenes tended to decrease feelings of anger and aggression, while urban scenes tended to increase them. Urban scenes also increased levels of loneliness and sadness; ironic considering that we are surrounded by fellow humans in cityscapes.

We can partly associate our mental states with what is going on inside the brain, so Ulrich began to delve deeper into the mechanisms and activity inside our neurology. In particular he began to examine brainwaves. When we are at work or really focused on an activity, the dominant brainwave pattern is beta waves. Beta waves are very quick and can operate up to thirty cycles per second. What this means is that if you were to look at the speed of information passing around the brain, along with its own processing, neutrons are firing up and connecting very quickly. Think about how your head felt the last time you were really busy; that's what beta waves feel like. We're answering phone calls, thinking about emails and generally multitasking at a very busy pace. Beta waves are also linked with higher levels of stress. When we are rested and relaxed, however, an EEG, or electroencephalograph, which measures brainwaves, would show up predominantly alpha wave patterns. Alpha waves can be as slow as four cycles per second and we experience them just before we go to sleep. If we are experiencing slower alpha waves, then most likely we are not in a stressed state.

Ulrich's research showed that people who were immersed in nature settings had a higher rate of alpha waves. These are the brainwaves that meditators experience and are associated with feelings of calmness and serenity. Serotonin levels rise when we experience alpha waves and this neurotransmitter is associated with feeling happy. Elderly patients in residential care homes also reported the same effects when shown nature scenes and their stress levels decreased as their alpha wave levels increased. A variety of scenes can stimulate alpha waves, from forests and orchards to rivers, streams and farmland settings. When participants were shown pictures of nature there was a noted preference for scenes that featured water in the form of lakes, rivers or streams. People preferred pictures that had between 33 and 66 per cent of water in the composition.

Fear vs Care

Well before psychiatric drugs and talk therapy became the default response to mental health issues, hospitals in the 1920s and 1930s were exploring the effect of water on mental health. Hydrotherapy was a standard practice for mental healthcare in the absence of psychotropic medication. Physicians used immersion in warm and cold baths as a form of therapy, along with steam showers and water vapour experiences. These therapies were used for treating depression, anxiety and mental exhaustion with varying degrees of success. To a lesser extent, contemporary researchers are still turning to hydrotherapy to consider its effects on the central nervous system. Immersion in warm baths facilities the move from activity in the sympathetic nervous system to activation of the parasympathetic nervous system or from fight or flight to rest and digest.

Neuroscience is still at an early stage in terms of its complete understanding of how the human brain works; yet particular regions are associated with particular emotional and mental states. Researchers in Korea began to look at the brain when participants were looking at nature and urban scenes via fMRI. Functional magnetic resonance imaging (fMRI) measures brain activity by measuring levels of blood flow throughout the brain. It relies on the premise that blood flow and neural activity are linked. So, if a participant is shown a picture of a natural landscape and blood flows to a particular region of the brain, then we can say that natural settings activate that particular part of the brain. The same can be said of the activation of brain regions when looking at urban settings.

When people were shown pictures of urban settings there was an increase of blood to the amygdala. The amygdala can continuously activate this response throughout the day without us being even consciously aware of these instinctive reactions. Interestingly, in other research, children were shown pictures of reptiles that they had never seen previously, and the exact same region fired up. It seems that we are wired to be afraid of anything that seems threatening even if we don't consciously know or understand the threat. This region of the brain is often called the rogue amygdala because it can set off stress responses to things that aren't really a threat. Streets and office tower blocks are not a threat to our survival, but it's difficult to teach this to the ancient part of the brain. It's like a guard dog that starts to bark when someone approaches our house at night, which is useful. Unfortunately, this particular guard dog keeps barking well into the night, long after the threat has disappeared. To a large extent, its activation and responses are outside of our control, so it's helpful to know the settings that make it feel safest. Basically, we don't feel very threatened in nature. Except for storms when we stay indoors anyway, the natural world of forests and seashore and meadows is non-threatening. It is a bath of calm for the stressed-out amygdala lost in a sea of data, demands and decisions.

Over-activation of the amygdala leads us to believe that the world is a scary place and can lead to anxiety, withdrawal and even depression. Research into green therapy shows that we can begin to assuage and control the amygdala, to some extent, by placing ourselves in environments where it feels that the human body is free from danger or harm. Over time, through practices like meditation, the amygdala can actually shrink in size and become less responsive. When the amygdala becomes less activated, other regions of the brain, such as the anterior cingulate and the insula, become more responsive and activated. These regions fire up on the fMRI when we are shown pictures of nature and these are also the regions that we use when we want to feel empathy or love for another. They are also intrinsically linked to altruistic behaviour.

When the amygdala is activated we are in survival mode and basically the brain is completely focused on how to get us away from danger. This is quite simply not a time to be thinking about others. Stressed people are known to be less empathetic or aware of the needs of those around them. This can be blamed on the brain because if you are running away from a chasing marauding tiger, it's not beneficial to stop to think about how your friend or tribal member is faring. Thinking about others in stressful situations lowers the odds on surviving. So when we are stressed, the empathetic and altruistic regions of our brain are effectively switched off. Again, blame the rogue amygdala. Stressful workplaces are, therefore, places where people can be somewhat immune to the feelings or needs of others as each individual is simply trying their best to survive and cater for their own needs. Unfortunately, our ability to be empathetic is somewhat on the decrease. Studies in America show that levels of empathy, or the ability to show concern when someone is in distress, have decreased by almost 50 per cent since the 1980s.

Screen Time — The New Stressor

In their book *Your Brain On Nature,* Eva M. Selhub and Alan C. Logan detail the detrimental effects of screen time on the human brain. They situate their findings in the context of the health benefits of time spent in nature. They note that in the past the lure of a cybernetic future promised humans a twenty-hour week, as computers would take over many of our tasks. For many, the opposite is true, as technology has now brought our workload right into the home. Currently 75 per cent of eighteen to forty-four year olds check work- or study-related emails while on their holidays. They link our dependence on screen time to higher levels of mental health disorders, along with childhood learning and behavioural disorders. Stress itself is responsible for many of our mental and physical health issues.

Research shows that video gaming and social media content lowers academic performance and memorisation scores in children and, overall, the time that we spend on screens lowers our cognitive performances. Selhub and Logan also cite a 2011 study of 4,500 adults where screen time was associated with higher risk of death. The increase was over 50 per cent. Time spent watching technological devices, be they smartphones, LED screens or TVs, reduces life expectancy. They claim that its effects are comparable with obesity and a lack of exercise. Screen time also affects our ability to be helpful to others and altruistic. Environmental overload caused by technology in the workplace leads to greater levels of insensitivity and the propensity to impulsively react to others. The correlative of a lack of altruism is an increase in narcissistic and self-absorbed behaviours. The people who scored the highest on narcissistic personality tests were also those who used Facebook the most. It is worth noting that altruism and compassion not only serve others but they are also characteristics that can lead to greater levels of inner contentedness and well-being.

Selhub and Logan put forward a nature displacement theory whereby we have abandoned time in nature in favour of time spent on screens. They refer to statistics which show that time spent in nature as a recreational activity has decreased by up to 50 per cent. Older generations will recall a childhood spent almost exclusively outdoors when playing, exploring and socialising with peers constituted a normal day, especially during holidays. They argue that screen time has now replaced time in nature and various statistics back this up with figures suggesting that teenagers now spend between seven and nine hours in front of screens per day. Many years ago, when there were no screens except the television, we were probably playing outdoors instead. Our addiction to screens is partly down to how the brain is wired. Our ancestors needed food and water to survive but they needed knowledge and information in order to find these precious supplies. For example, the waft of geosmin in the air was vital information and the brain rewards this new data acquisition with a shot of dopamine. Information increased our chances of survival yet now we find ourselves living in an information highway where streams of data are reaching us every moment of every day on a variety of platforms. A typical smartphone can have 64 gigabytes of storage, which can store many years of photos and personal videos. In a typical day, our brains are now being bombarded with over 70 gigabytes of information, a complete overload. If our evolution was a twenty-four-hour clock, we have just arrived into towns and cities in the last few minutes. We have only started watching screens in the last few seconds. Our brains are completely overwhelmed in the modern world and the price we pay is greater levels of stress and anxiety.

When we find out new information about events around the world and the latest updates about our friends and colleagues from social media platforms we get a dopamine hit. This is addictive and we stay on our screens, awash with this neurotransmitter. It would be handy if the brain punished us for spending time on our screens and rewarded us for being outside but it doesn't work that way. Neural systems compete with each other and it is up to us to decide which activity is best for our health and higher self. It is up to us where we pay our attention. The brain will reward us for going outside in nature and it will reward us for seeking out new information, which it deems necessary for survival. It is up to each individual to decide which activity is best for them. The brain is not fixed and it will create new neural pathways depending on where we put our attention. It's like a muscle that gets stronger every time we use it. This is called neural plasticity. Pathways that are repeatedly activated become strengthened.

Remember, we are all living with a rogue amygdala so the higher self always has to make the decision as to what's best. Even though we've been praising the health benefits of being with trees, up to two thousand people get lost in the woods every year. Unfortunately, many don't survive. In those instances, a love of nature and its health benefits needed to be balanced and corrected with knowledge of the woods. Sometimes the dopamine hit is a good thing, and can be the difference between life and death.

Neural Networks and Nature's Balance

There are basically two main networks in our brain, the central executive network and the default mode network. The executive network is located more at the front part of our brains, which is also the most evolved region. We use this part when we are engaged in our daily activities, especially when we are at work. A lot of the time we use the executive network in an involuntary way. This means that we are being asked to do our daily tasks at work and at home and they are simply things we just have to do. We have to attend to the daily practical demands of human life. Our ancestors also used this part of their brains to hunt and search for food and seek protection. The difference for our forebears was that they also got a lot of time to take a rest from using this network. Neural networks are organic and get worn out if we use them too much. Unfortunately we use our executive network for a huge proportion of the day because when we're not working most of us go onto our screens for downtime. The result is that many of us are now suffering from direct attention fatigue. It's like that feeling when our eyes get tired in front of our screens. We rub our foreheads, literally because that part of our brain is exhausted and worn out. Our thoughts live along organic neural networks and it is easy to wear these out, especially given our habit of turning to our screens for a bit of diversion.

The second network is the default network, and is located more in the back region of the brain. So, when we are not engaged with some activity that is demanding our attention, we slip into the default network of thoughts, feelings and daydreams. This is the part of the brain that switches on when the executive network switches off. It is the location of fantasy, daydreaming and what's sometimes referred to as the me-me-

me network. It is basically where we think about ourselves. This in itself is not a bad thing, if life is really good. The mental health continuum would show that we are happy, creative and generally thriving. But if life is not so good and we find ourselves on the other end of the continuum where we are anxious, stressed or even depressed then this network becomes the location for brooding and ruminating thoughts. It can even become nightmarish if life is really challenging. It is where we get caught in loops of overthinking tiny life scenarios located in the past or the future. We brood on mistakes in the past or ruminate on possible things that might go wrong in the future.

Both networks can be really happy places when life is good but, unfortunately, many in the Western fast-paced technological world find that life is pressured and stressed and even much of their off time feels overwrought. In that instance, both of these networks are burdened by overactivity and lack the balance that our forebears might have enjoyed. Each network needs to be regulated so that it can be rested and reset. And it just so happens that this is where nature really comes to our aid.

We spoke about how nature can evoke feelings of awe and wonder. What's wonderful about green landscapes is that they have the ability to draw our attention out of those two networks into a sort of middle zone that operates somewhere between the two. The type of thinking in this middle zone is sometimes referred to as 'soft fascination'. It acts almost in seesaw fashion between the two networks. As such, it doesn't over rely on either, thus giving them both a rest. When we are in nature we find that we are paying attention to our natural surroundings, exploring, listening and observing movement. But it's of a voluntary nature. This means we want to pay attention to the blues and the greens because they don't place any demands on us. Nature doesn't ask us to do anything. It just lets us be. So we can use a part of our executive network but we're also using a part of the default network. We are immersed in nature, but also in a slight daydream state or restful observation. Research shows that when we are in nature, we are less likely to brood on worries or troubles. We are in our natural home where there's simply less to worry about. Rachel and Stephen Kaplan formulated the 'attention restoration theory' in the early 1980s, which explained how nature could heal the mental fatigue that is responsible for many mental and physical health issues. Something like forest bathing is like washing both of these networks with a refreshing and renewing balm of greens and blues. It is the location of soft fascination. Here the networks are restored by birdsong and the smells of pine and cedar wood and maybe the scent of geosmin in the damp, rain-washed earth. We will apply their theory to a practical natural setting in the practices section at the end of part three.

Green Exercise

Due to the fact that most of us live in urban settings, an amount of movement is required before we can immerse ourselves in nature. Many of us couple our time in woodland or shoreline with some amount of physical exercise. Time spent in nature is good for us but one of the reasons for this is that when we are roaming the fields or hiking, we are also getting some exercise. Aerobic activity has been prescribed for millennia as a therapeutic tool from Roman civilisations to Chinese medicinal practice. Exercise in the form of tai chi or chi kung has been the bedrock of Chinese medicine for thousands of years. These ancient practices cultivate an attitude to medicine where health comes before healing. If we physically exercise, we can ward off many physical and mental illnesses. In Western medicine, we can sometimes wait for something to go wrong before we try to heal it. In some Chinese medicine practices, on the other hand, the health practitioner gets paid to keep people well. He or she stops being paid when people get sick. Physical exercise has always been harnessed as part of their armoury against illness and fatigue.

Research is now showing that exercise has a positive effect on mental health and can act as an antidepressant or anti-anxiety agent. Selhub and Logan cite research of ten thousand young adults where those who spent most of their time on a screen had a 30 per cent higher chance of developing a mental illness. On the other hand, those who pursued active and consistent physical exercise had a 28 per cent less chance of developing a mental disorder. One of the reasons that exercise promotes mental health is because it increases our levels of serotonin and dopamine, the mood-regulating neurotransmitters that make us feel better. Exercise strengthens our cardiovascular health but also has antioxidant and anti-inflammatory effects and reduces the chemicals attributed to depressive tendencies. It is worth noting that serotonin is produced in two bundles of neurons located deep in the brainstem called the serotonin raphe nuclei. These little factories produced a generous output for our ancestors as they spent most of their time in nature, in the soil and in sunlight. Over time our brains grew much larger but the raphe nuclei never increased in size. This means that it is much easier for us to suffer from depletion of serotonin than our forebears. This points even more to the importance of interventions like exercise to help regulate our levels of this mood enhancer.

Exercise reduces stress and inflammation provided it's regular and consistent. A bout of exercise on the body can cause harm if the body is not ready and prepared for it. The brain is an anticipatory organ and likes to know what's about to happen next. So to get the best benefits from exercise, we should adopt exercise patterns that we will actually stick to, instead of ones that are placed upon us. For best results, we should also engage with the type of exercise that we enjoy the most, be it walking, swimming or running. The simple act of walking is shown to increase cognitive function in both the young and the old. Walking for two miles per day can reduce the risk of dementia in older people while even a twenty-minute walk can increase resiliency and cognitive performance in teenagers.

In *The Well Gardened Mind,* Sue Stuart-Smith likens the neural processes in a healthy brain to the activity of a gardener. She focuses on a group of cells, numbering about one in every ten neurons, that take on the job of weeding, pruning and removing obsolete cells in our brains. These cells, called microglial cells, operate in tiny neural localities, a bit like gardeners cultivating their own patch of land. They are highly mobile, as they root out redundant cells and fertilise new cells. It is a process called neurogenesis and is intrinsic to the regenerative processes

| Pruned vines.

in our brains. Our brains change and adapt to new experiences and data, but these cells create our new mindsets and thought processes at the cellular level. Our thoughts live along these neural networks so if we want new thoughts, we have to support these little gardeners of the mind. The fertiliser that microglial cells use is called brain-derived neurotrophic factor or BDNF. Low levels of BDNF have been linked to depression. Levels of this protein are increased through exercise and especially through the activity of the muscles in our legs.

When we suffer from anxiety or depression our whole brains cannot function properly. Small neural networks or loops become dominant and we feel like we are in a rut. We cannot seem to escape particular and unwanted pathways of thinking. The process of pruning away old neural networks and uprooting old thought patterns simply isn't happening. This may be due to low levels of the proteins needed for neurogenesis.

This is why exercise is linked to better mental health. Studies have shown that outdoor exercise in woodlands is better for us because the surfaces we run or walk along are uneven and unpredictable. Obviously we don't want to trip or fall over so the whole brain becomes very active in outdoor activities in order to keep us safe. It is this very whole-brain activity that is beneficial for our mental health. If we are caught up in a loop of anxious or depressive thinking, the other parts of our brain can't offer perspectives or alternatives. Regular exercise, especially outdoors, strengthens the circuitry of the whole brain, thus competing with narrower and myopic depressive thought patterns. The brain is an energy-efficient organ and will not invest its resources in new circuitry unless it's going to be used. That's why we need to exercise regularly so that we can persuade the brain that it is worthwhile to invest in new neural pathways.

Positive mental health is dependant upon our thought processes so anything that improves them or regenerates them is to be welcomed. Study after study links improved mental health with exercise and, though it may not come as a surprise, exercise outdoors in nature is even better than exercise in the gym. People are more inclined to exercise outdoors rather than indoors simply because it makes them feel better. Exercise in wooded areas supersedes exercise in level open areas. It appears that we benefit more from environments that provide greater variety as they induce that state of soft fascination. We are drawn from the world of our own ruminating into the heterogeneity and diversification of sound, light and texture in the surrounding landscape. Doctor Li has shown that forest exercise elevated mood and vitality in participants while decreasing fatigue, tension and cortisol levels. Interestingly, landscapes with blue and green score even higher; so, if the sun is shining, get going in the great outdoors. As previously noted, Dr Li has also shown that sleep is improved after time spent in nature. Neurogenesis is at its most productive during sleep because our brain shrinks slightly allowing the microglial cells to roam around with their gardening tools, freer and less hindered.

Labyrinths are now used in schools and hospitals to promote calmness and well-being. Walking the labyrinth allows us to slow down and the design also supports whole-brain activity.

An important caveat that we need to add to green exercise relates to harmonising the self to the patterns and movement in nature. A powerful tincture that nature applies to our stressed minds is the prescription to slow down both physically and mentally. It is important to slow down to a saunter or standstill after walking briskly or running through an outdoor setting because slowing down is really good mental training. The problem with our neurological physiology is that the thalamus gets to react instantaneously to incoming data. It is governed by the hypervigilant amygdala so we often react to benign or inane data as if it were a threat. Basically, we go with our immediate reactions instead of waiting for the data to be processed by our executive network located around our frontal lobes. It takes about half a second for incoming data to reach this region, which allows our higher self to analyse data and respond accordingly; for example, when we see a coiled piece of tubing on the ground, the thalamus will initially get us to react as if it's a snake. We immediately go into a stress response. If we slow down, the executive network will accurately identify it as a piece of tubing and walk on.

This ability to slow down mental responses is an evolved response that we are only beginning to utilise. Relax and respond is a superior way of going about our daily tasks compared to fight or flight. We are stressing up in response to far too much incoming data when we don't need to. How often do we get angry with other motorists for being too slow when in fact we weren't in a hurry anyway? How often do we react impulsively and impatiently to family members and co-workers when a more reasoned response would have relaxed the situation? Technological overload can exacerbate impulsive reactions, which often worsen situations and get us in trouble. We 'fly off the handle' or 'lose the head'. When we are in nature we can train both the physical and mental body to slow down. We can walk really slowly looking left and right, thus promoting that healthy whole-brain activity. We can enter that state of soft fascination where we enjoy the slower mental processing and some attention restoration. So after fast exercise always try to slow down and move slowly. When situations arise in daily life also try to slow down the speed of your reactions to allow for the higher processing of relax and respond.

In nature we need to train ourselves by slowing down all our movements, walking, sitting, reaching and looking. The results of this training can then be brought back into our busier home or work environments and we can start to replace impulsive reactions with relaxed responses. It is in this manner that we slowly begin to evolve our own inner workings, which in turn will lead to less stress and anxiety in daily life. The best way to utilise green therapy is by bringing the experiences and sensations that it teaches us back into the grey life of the city or urban landscapes. Greening the grey is like a muscle and the more we train ourselves by being in nature, the stronger it gets. Designers of shopping malls have also discovered that greenery slows down our movements. They've discovered that shoppers slow down in areas where there are lots of plants and flowers. Accordingly, they also spend more in those areas. So the next time you see some plants strategically placed in a shopping area, buyer beware!

| The Woods.

The Story of the Soil

Another form of exercise is to work in the garden, cultivating and minding a patch of soil. If we dig, turn, prepare and help compost a piece of soil, it in turn will nourish us. This is a central principle of green therapy: when we take care of the soil, it takes care of us; when we heal the soil, it heals us. When it comes to mental health issues the hearty soil of the earth has many messages to tell us. We just need to slow down a little bit to decipher her language of symbol and metaphor. Remember, we are *Adamah* and *humus* so sometimes the processes in the soil can mirror our mental and emotional processes.

The soil has a message for those who might feel less than others and who believe that they are not enough. The soil has a message for those who think that mental health issues are a type of personal failure. She speaks from her peaty brown womb to those who have lost hope and have given up on life because soil is unlike any other substance on the planet. It is the giver of all life but it is also the receptacle of sickness and death. Everything that cannot develop fully, the misshapen, the weak sprouts, the withered stalks, all make their way back into the soil. That which is healthy and strong takes from the soil. That which is dying, sickly and weak gives to the soil. The soil, unlike anything else, needs death and decay to renew and replenish its resources, the same way a dead tree supports more life than a living one.

The coarse brown furrows of the earth are subversive to the way we understand what human needs to be. The world lauds success and abhors failure. The world demands perfection and punishes imperfection. It celebrates hard work and productivity and shuns the unproductive. Those who experience mental health issues often cannot do much in the way of work and creativity. They are simply minding themselves. Sickness and illnesses of any type are important moments on the journey of human life and they can be intense times of personal growth. The Swiss psychologist Carl Jung said that humans need suffering and challenges and that they were necessary for psychological health.

The soil tells us that the tomb of the dead is in fact the womb of new life. All root tips feed on the processes of fungal decay and rot. What withers and appears lifeless disappears into the alchemy of decomposition and growth. The challenges that life gives us, the experiences of loss, meaninglessness and suffering, when treated properly, are in fact intrinsic to the journey of self-understanding. If we hold onto the notion of who we are and stubbornly reject change, we can stultify into stagnation and stunt our own growth. The soil needs a cycle of life and death, growth and decay or else it cannot survive. The experience of mental health issues often makes us feel like we are not flourishing but the cycles of the soil tell us that weakness, melancholy and failure are part of the stuff and substance of life.

That which decays and dies enters into the crucible of the soil to be transmuted into life in the same way that our mental health issues are part of a journey towards healing and health. The growth patterns in the earth say a healthy and hearty yes to all the living processes and all of the dying processes. The growth patterns of the human psyche also need all the living processes and all of the dying processes of human experience. The healthy soil and the healthy psyche reject nothing, and can happily feed off everything. The clay in our hands says to us that it is quite okay not to feel okay. It is okay to be stressed, anxious or depressed because those experiences are part of a cycle that includes well-being, greater resilience and human flourishing. A single teaspoon of soil can contain up to seven billion different organisms, including thousands of species of fungi, bacteria and protozoa. It screams life and growth from every tiny square milligram of microbial mayhem. Without the nourishment of this cacophony of dirt and darkness, all plant life would eventually die. Soon afterwards all human life on this planet would perish and be extinguished. So there is life in mayhem, hope in darkness, growth in chaos. What's true for the soil is also true for human.

Green Therapy

In recent years psychotherapists and psychiatrists have begun to embrace the possibilities offered by moving their sessions with patients and clients outdoors. A study published in *Psychiatry Investigation* in 2009 reported on the effects of moving therapy sessions outdoors. Sixty-three patients were sampled and the group was split, with some continuing their therapy in the hospital setting while others were immersed in the forest setting of an arboretum. The results showed the most significant reduction in depressive symptoms for the forest group. The odds of a complete remission were also raised by about 30 per cent in the outdoor group. This group also showed lower levels of cortisol and higher heart rate variability, which is a marker for activity in the parasympathetic nervous system. Therapy entails a level of cognitive engagement on the part of the patient but we find it hard to direct our attention to processing information and questions if we are in a stressed state. The fight or flight system doesn't have time for therapy sessions as it's trying to escape from a predator so one possibility is that the arboretum allowed the patients to relax more, thus enabling the cognitive processes that therapy entails.

Nature also allows the mind to get out of the cognitive loops caused by anxiety, stress and depression. It induces whole-brain activity, which allows the patient to become creative and solution orientated. The fight or flight response is solution focused but in a very myopic way, literally trying to figure out whether to run up a tree or jump across a stream. To get ourselves out of depressive or anxious states, the brain has to operate differently and ultimately it has to become creative as we attempt to build a new relationship with the world around us. The safety of the natural world allows the stressed or fear-based brain to relinquish its hold on narrow survival mechanisms in order to engage with new thought patterns.

In 2006 Dutch health scientist Dr Peter P. Groenewegen applied the term 'vitamin G' to the medicinal use of green space. Doctors and therapists are now beginning to actively write prescriptions for vitamin G where you go to a forest, park or seashore instead of a pharmacy. These prescriptions detail specified amounts of exercise and time to spend in nature, along with mindfulness exercises to facilitate a better engagement with plants, animals and trees. Research continuously shows that those who are most stressed have the most to gain from being in nature but they are also the people who find it hardest to get time outdoors, hence the need to be actually given a written prescription from a doctor. The best prescriptions for vitamin G include a range of different but specific activities so that the patient will know that they have taken their medication. The practical tips sections at the end of each part of this book provide a useful range of activities that could form part of a prescription for vitamin G. Ultimately, though, rest, mindfulness and solitude form the essential ingredients of any session of green therapy.

9. Wondering and Wandering

The research and science behind green therapy is still at an early stage and there are still many unanswered questions as to exactly why it is that nature is so good for us. How can we fully explain why the phytoncides and terpenes that swirl amongst the crowns of trees boost our immunity? Why do our eyes scan our world in the exact same fractal patterns that we find in ferns, trees and sunflowers? We know that the smell of essential oils in conifer trees boosts our mood and makes us feel less anxious but how did it come to be this way? And why do oaks send nutrients to a five-hundred-year-old great-ancestor to keep it alive? Can trees relate to each other or can only humans have relationships? If trees can relate to each other, can they relate to us? If so, what exactly is the nature of that relationship? Do trees intentionally help us out or is it merely accidental? Maybe it is best to leave it to the reader to fully answer these questions for themselves. Everyone has a different way of relating to the natural world and there can be as many different answers to that question are there are humans on the planet. The purpose of this book, in part, has been to make sure that the questions stay alive and maybe we can even create a few new ones.

We may not be able to describe exactly the nature of our relationship with the natural world to the satisfaction of all but a relationship does exist and if we ignore it we can damage each other. If we ignore the needs of the earth, as we have done, we damage her.

Yet when we damage the earth, we damage ourselves. As we have seen, the earth can act as our healer so if we damage her, we are damaging our therapist and our source of free therapy. When Robin Kimmerer studied the relationship between humans and nature she examined how we cultivate sweetgrass. She discovered that it flourishes when we harvest it in proper proportions. If we over harvest it, it dies. If we harvest it just the right amount, the thinning helps it to strengthen and multiply. She advocates a honourable harvest, a symbiotic relationship of mutual caring and sharing. The rewilding that is advocated in the We Are The Ark project can actually only work properly if a human is present to remove invasive species that are not native to the patch of ground under our care. Nature needs us and we need nature.

Down to Earth

Humans are born wanderers and explorers and an illuminating insight into the health benefits that the earth provides comes from our first forays into space travel. Physiological effects from the absence of gravity include a loss of bone density, which also led to muscle wastage. After five months in space, a twenty-year-old body can resemble a sixty year old in terms of muscle atrophy. Some of the effects of space can be explained, others will require decades more research. One interesting theory, however, suggests that astronauts also suffer in the absence of what's sometimes referred to as 'the earth's heartbeat' or the Schumann resonance. In 1953 Professor W.O. Schumann of the University of Munich discovered that the earth created its own frequency or pulse. Lightning hits the earth about fifty times every second and there can be up to two thousand thunderstorms pummelling the planet at any given time. This electrical activity sends waves sixty miles up into the ionosphere and their frequency has been measured somewhere to between 6 and 8 hertz.

The Schumann resonance can be found anywhere on the planet but we find it difficult to detect because it doesn't have a strong amplitude.

The reason that this resonance is so interesting for humans is because it is made up of alpha waves, which can also be found in our brains when we are relaxed or at rest. We find beta waves in our brains when we are stressed but alpha waves when we are relaxed. The Schumann resonance is ideally suited to humans as it can induce a more relaxed state. Unfortunately all of the electronic equipment in our lives quashes the effects of earth's own pulse. If, on the other hand, we can get ourselves away from electronic frequencies, we can attune ourselves to the more calming frequency of the earth. Needless to say, the best way to tune into the earth's resonance and pulse is by venturing out into the natural landscape, as far away from wires, masts and mobile phones as we can get. This theory also goes someway towards explaining why we feel calmer and more relaxed when we are out in nature, bathed in the earth's own alpha waves.

In many religious traditions it was deemed necessary to take off one's shoes when entering sacred ground. If we were to treat our time in nature as sacred, we could go barefoot all the time, human skin on earth's bare soil. Walking barefoot on the earth brings us into direct contact with the earth's vibration, restoring the brain and mind to renewing and creative alpha waves. Due to the barrage of lightning strikes, the earth holds a negative electrical charge while most humans carry a positive charge. There is a theory that this positive charge can cause us problems especially with inflammation, fatigue and some cases of chronic disease. When we come into direct contact with the earth in our bare feet, our bodies are conductively connected with the electrical charge of the earth's surface. The process of grounding, or earthing, allows for a flow of the earth's electrons onto our bodies and in so doing it stabilises our electrical environment. People who practise grounding on a regular basis report that their sleep improves and levels of pain from old or new injuries are lessened. Many studies have been done on this practice and more need to be done but the research does point to tantalising evidence that both the frequency and electrical charge of our planet are beneficial for the human body.

Harmony

'Biophilia' is a term that was first coined by the American psychoanalyst Erich Fromm. It refers to the urge in humans to be connected to all living things and the whole of the natural world. This connection has evolved over millions of years and the theory is that we still long to be in a relationship of some kind with our green spaces. We have ancient green roots that cannot penetrate the grey concrete of our cityscapes. Instead we need to find grounding in the soft soil of our gardens and the earth. Our immune system and mood does not appear to get a boost while walking along the street but it does when we are ambling along a forest path.

As we have demonstrated, there is a great benefit to be had for humans when we connect and harmonise ourselves with the earth and her natural rhythms. When we wander barefoot on an old, worn track through a meadow to the woods, our internal electrical systems resonate with the electromagnetic systems surrounding the planet. Yet we need to immerse ourselves in nature long enough for these subtle changes to occur. Whilst standing in a meadow or at the edge of the forest we need to really smell, touch, breathe and listen for the healing to occur. We need to recalibrate our relationship with nature so as to become one with it.

When a fox in the forest looks at us, she sees no distinction between us and an otter that is sauntering by a stream. When the otter looks at us, he sees no distinction between us and the fox. For both these animals we are simply other living creatures occupying the forest space. If aliens were to visit from outer space and hover over the planet for the first time, they would simply count us as one species among the others. We may be more advanced in some respects and enjoy a higher level of consciousness, but we are just living creatures roaming this tract of blue and green like any others. Any sense of greater importance that we might have comes from ourselves. It does not come from foxes, sparrows and otters.

When we successfully invert the hierarchical typologies in our own minds we cease to control nature and instead become part of it. This is a vital rethinking and reconceptualisation of who and what we are if we are to benefit from nature. We cannot heal our worn-out human systems with nature's replenishing systems if we are not harmonised with it. We cannot consume or purchase these remedies; instead we have to spend time slowing down and immersing ourselves in her energies. As we relinquish ourselves to her hidden wisdom and energy, we cease to try to control her but instead flow and pulse in unison with her archaic rhythms and patterns. It is then that there is real communication back and forth between these two living systems sharing this planet. Each listens and responds to the needs of the other. Nature stimulates our immunity because we need it. Yet in this moment as we stand still to get our green prescription, we might notice some damage that we have caused her. We might notice a damaged ecosystem and take steps to repair and restore with acts of kindness. Green therapy can only work both ways and it needs to work in both ways. If we don't take care of our healer, our healer will diminish, wilt and die. We need to think of ourselves as part of a wood wide web through which we barter with nature in order to stay relevant and needed. It takes and it gives and in response we take and we give. As the forest breathes out, we breathe in. As we breathe out, the forest breathes in.

Our relationship with nature might be best understood as symbiotic. When we create wild spaces for ecosystems to restore themselves we have to root out invasive species. As we reach into the earth to do this careful weeding, we ground and earth ourselves, thus restoring and balancing our own electromagnetic systems. As we plant native trees in the earth, we boost our immunity and gut health by breathing in and touching healthy soil bacteria. As we abandon our need to control a corner of our property to the innate blueprint of the soil, we can rest ourselves and softly listen to birdsong. As native seedlings get a chance to root and sprout, our nervous system gets a chance to self-regulate. It is simple. When we heal her, she heals us. When we listen to her, she listens to us. Ecological sustainability applies to all of the species that roam the earth and that includes our species. If we continue to try to control nature, we cannot be in harmony with it. If we are not in

Solitary bees like to burrow little holes to live in south-facing sandy banks. They need humans to clear the banks for them or else it is too difficult to burrow through the vegetation into the sand.

harmony with it, we cannot be healed by it. We are part of a whole and when one part of it is sick and damaged, it is all sick and damaged. It is in the interest of this whole planet that when one part of it needs healing, be it a human or a forest, the other parts will provide that remedy. This is why the word 'whole' has its roots in the Old English words 'healthy', 'healing' and 'safe'.

Old Friends

Studies show that those of us who spent most of our time in nature as children, playing and exploring, end up with more interest in the environment as adults. Children who are being taught about the health benefits of nature are also the ones who promote a more sustainable lifestyle. The research shows that once we learn and experience the remedies that the outdoors can give us, we respond by protecting the environment and living more sustainably. If we want to teach our children to care for the environment, we need to begin by teaching them how the environment cares for them. Children now spend up to 50 per cent less time outdoors than their parents and grandparents and in most cases even spend less time outdoors than prisoners. The great ecological challenges that face them could best be met by teaching them the myriad of ways that the earth can enhance their mental, physical and emotional health; for example, green therapy is increasingly being promoted in the treatment of ADHD as children who experience this condition thrive when they are taught outdoors. Astronauts in space sometimes experience a cognitive shift in awareness called the overview effect. It comes from being able to view the earth from outer space and commonly they become more aware of how tiny and fragile the planet appears in the context of the vastness of space. This is our only home and we have to reconnect with her to save her. In so doing, we save ourselves. We are not only old friends with the bacteria in our gut. We are old friends with the natural world in its entirety. It is a symbiotic friendship that mutually supports and strengthens each part and species. As we have seen, there are ancient regions of our neurology that actually miss our green home. The wide-open savannah was nature's way of saying we were safe. The sounds of a gurgling brook or lake water lapping were auditory signals that we could lie down and rest. The scent of geosmin in the air assuaged the fear of a threat of thirst. Birdsong once woke us up and then washed our bodies with feel-good chemicals. Drenched forests in sunlight elevated our mood and the damp earth underfoot grounded, rooted and secured us. There are many threats in the world but nature is not one of them. That green home is our safe place.

After creation, the first thing that God did was to name things. Naming things was also the first responsibility that Nanabozho was given by his creator. We do not know the names of strangers, that's what makes them strange, but we know the names of our friends, that's what makes them friends. When someone remembers our name it makes us feel secure and wanted. When someone forgets our name, it's the opposite. When we start to forget the names of our old friends in nature, philosophers refer to it as species loneliness. It's that strange sad feeling of estrangement, of never feeling fully at home. Familiar brand names adorn our street corners and shop windows but when a leaf falls from a tree, do we always know its name?

As we come to the end of this book, a good place to start is by beginning to learn how to name things again when we go outdoors.

This is how we can increase our vocabulary so as to be able to write our own green prescriptions. The dosages can vary but we recommend good amounts of sycamore, spruce, Scots pine and oak. Also try plenty of azaleas, dahlias, geraniums and chrysanthemums. Try not to forget garlic, ginger, ginseng and goldenseal. And when in season, try blueberries, raspberries, loganberries and blackberries. To name but a few.

The reader can decide on the strength and frequency of the dosage themselves but we recommend going barefoot at least once a week. For best results, take your prescription daily for at least five minutes, morning and evening. Try to get a dawn chorus of blackbird, chaffinch and thrush. In the evening look out for a murder of crows or a murmur of starlings. Side effects may include serenity, happiness and clarity of thought. There are many remedies for those who are sick, alone, depressed or unhappy but one of the best is to just go outside. Walk slowly if you can. Maybe find a seat. Simply breathe and then close your eyes. Let the tired bones and muscles of your body rest and relax. Let your limbs unwind. Let the mind settle, like still water. Then try your absolute best to do absolutely nothing.

Practical Tips

1. Harmonising

Nature teaches us about energy systems all the time: how to produce and how to rest. There is a seasonal blueprint for work and rest embedded in the flow and energy of the seasons. In order to harmonise ourselves with these patterns, we need to really slow down, stop sometimes and just observe. Like us, nature is alive, its ecosystems are created, live and die. Nature understands how energy works and when we become one with it there is much to learn.

- When we have been busy, it is hard to slow down, stop even, and look properly at what is going on in nature. It is important to stop moving and become still so as to really observe the seasonal patterns of growth and rest. Stop and look left and right as this activates whole-brain activity, which can get us out of those small ruminating loops of thinking.

- Practise walking and sitting down slowly. Try to reach out and touch something as slowly as you can. Let your breathing slow down. See how slowly you can reach a destination instead of how quickly you can do it. This is one way we can train ourselves to shift from the fight or flight response to the relax and respond response in everyday activities.

- Creating thresholds can help. Mark the place where you leave behind the ordinary world and where you make the crossing into the world of green therapy. Walk slowly, find a seat or 'shed' to sit in. Let your breathing settle. Let your mind settle. Allow your brain to move into soft-fascination mode.

- All year around, try to notice which season you are in and which part of the season. Autumn and winter give us permission to rest and to learn how to do that throughout the year. It reminds us to let go of that which needs to be let go. Spring and summer harvests celebrate productivity and newness and give us permission to change, grow and create.

- Visit wilderness areas as much as possible as they are one of the most beneficial natural landscapes we can immerse ourselves in. These places are not judged nor have attempts been made to change them. They're just allowed to rest and be the way they are. The world is full of judgement and we can be filled with self-judgement, so sometimes the message of the wilderness is what we need to hear for ourselves: it's okay not to be okay; it's okay to be you, exactly the way you are.

2. Creativity

Earlier we identified the Schumann resonance or heartbeat of the earth. The earth's own frequency creates alpha waves that can be picked up if we are out in nature and away from electronic devices. Alpha waves are also the best frequency for the brain to operate on if it is trying to be creative because they support whole-brain activity. Creativity is really about joining things together to create something new so placing ourselves in the peace and quiet of nature is one of the best things we can do to promote imagination and innovative thinking. The best manual on human creativity can be read by simply watching the natural patterns of growth and creativity in nature itself. Just as there are four seasons, we can identify four phases in the dynamics of harnessing our own creative potential:

- Clearing: We can't control creativity. We can form and hold an intention for our lives but change may not work out exactly as we'd planned. The universe can sometimes work in mysterious and surprising ways. When we clear a piece of ground to plant something, many different things might also grow alongside it.

- Planting: Then we plant our own seeds. It is interesting to watch what we plant seed and sprout but it is also good to allow the earth to grow what it wants to grow. It's a symbiotic relationship. Weeds like dandelions are extremely nutritious and sustain bees. To be truly creative, we must accept that there's an amount we can control and an amount we can't control. Some weeding is necessary, some can be damaging to biodiversity.

- Incubation: Once we've prepared the ground and planted seeds there is a period of rest and incubation. This mirrors the neurological processes in creativity. We play with lots of ideas and then let them all incubate. The subconscious mind then works out what the best idea might be to go forward. This is sometimes referred to as the eureka moment. Then the idea, like a seed, breaks ground into our consciousness.

- Testing: Managing a plot of ground and clearing, planting and sowing is extremely therapeutic. There are so many hidden messages for the psyche in the unfolding growth patterns. To create one good idea we have to test and then weed out lots of ones that don't make it. Then we need to support the idea that is growing, nurture, feed and manage its growth. To be creative is a long process and supporting your idea from the harsh winds of criticism is important. Similarly, it's important to listen to other people's helpful criticism. This is when we test our idea and shape it, just like many plants need pruning as they grow.

3. Grounding

Grounding is the practice of going barefoot out in nature. The electrical charge of the earth helps to regulate the electrical charge in our bodies. Grounding can also operate at the level of our mental health because too often we can be caught up in the activity and ruminating going on in our head. Grounding can help to balance our energies as we focus on the earth instead of our thinking.

- We can ground ourselves anywhere outside. Rubber soles insulate us from the electromagnetic influence of the earth so once we remove this artificial membrane we can reconnect and earth ourselves. Shoes with natural leather soles are the best, however, for natural conductivity.
- Once we are rested and seated we can begin a very simple grounding exercise that can help us with mental fatigue brought about by all the thinking going on in our heads. We can start by closing our eyes and just allowing the breath to regulate. Take in the sounds for a while just to settle into the surroundings.
- Then, having allowed the body to settle and relax, slowly allow your attention to move down along your body until you reach your feet. Become aware of where your feet touch the earth, the sensations of this. This is your earthing or grounding point.
- You can then imagine slender roots coming out of your feet and entering into the soil. Remember the coolness and dampness of the earth the last time you had your hands in it. Imagine these energetic roots growing down into the earth about the same depth as your height; thus, we become balanced between our headspace and our rootedness. Allow the earth to nourish, renew and support you just as you support her. After a while bring your attention back up along your body and slowly open your eyes.

4. Greening the Grey

In this book we encountered research that shows how urban landscapes can raise our stress levels while green landscapes can lower them. It is important, therefore, to carry what we've learned outdoors into our indoors, streets, schools and office buildings. A significant part of our evolution is to learn how to live in grey spaces without getting stressed.

- If we are in nature and our minds and bodies feel refreshed, relaxed and calmer, it is possible to experience the same feelings back in our homes and workplaces. Nature will relax us; we don't have to *do* anything. Back in the city we need to make the effort but we can still get the same results. Practices like yoga and meditation and resting the body will all support the activity of the parasympathetic nervous system. Brain plasticity allows our brain to adapt to the urban or office landscape in a more evolved way with practice and training.

- Research shows that man-made noise like engines, machines and especially airplanes can lead to stress responses. A good practice is to sit in an urban landscape with your eyes closed and just listen to all of the noises around you. We can start to tell ourselves that these noises aren't threatening. We are safe listening to the traffic or industrial noises. This needs to be a conscious activity of softening our reaction to urban noises. We are part of nature and all that we build is part of nature so really we are just expanding the scope for what we term 'natural'.

- It is important to bring greenery into our work, living and school spaces. Try to have a view of greenery from where you work. Open your window and listen to birdsong in the morning and evening. Even forty seconds looking at a natural landscape can help our focus and attention. Just taking ten minutes to look at pictures of nature is enough to boost our cognitive performance. If you can't look at nature outside, then look at pictures. All of these micro-interventions are enough to help keep us calm, focused and alert.

- Decorate your living and working spaces with living plants. Take care of them, watering, feeding and pruning off dead leaves and flowers. All of plant life is a metaphor for us. How we take care of the soil and all that grows in it is how we ultimately take care of ourselves. Simply taking care of one plant can be a great catalyst for practising some self-care of our own.

5. The Story of Soil

Attempts have been made to try to plant exotic trees inside gigantic glasshouses in climates where they wouldn't normally grow. Often it doesn't work because the roots don't grow deep enough into the soil. Tree roots have been known to descend up to two hundred feet into the earth. Realising that the trees weren't rooting into the soil because they didn't need strong roots in such an artificial climate, their carers began shaking them to mimic storms and winds. The trees then began to root properly and to flourish. It would appear that the more we root ourselves and involve ourselves in soil, the more we thrive.

- If you can, clear a patch of soil in your garden so that you are just left with a tapestry of brown potential. When we look at soil, we are looking at one of the best metaphors for understanding human. So, in ways, you are peering into a mirror image of yourself. There are so many things to learn about yourself by simply attending to a piece of soil.

- Springtime is an excellent time to become involved with a piece of soil. It could even be a big pot in an apartment. Leave aside some of the soil to see what it wants to grow itself. This gives you permission to be the person you want to be as well. As we practise not controlling the soil, we give ourselves permission not to be controlled by others. We can also reflect on how much we try to control others. Remember, the solutions to the earth's ecological challenges lie in allowing the earth to do what it wants.

- Involve yourself in a variety of gardening activities. This involves sowing, planting, watering, pruning and thinning out. You also have to weed out invasive species of weeds, whilst allowing some to grow. As we watch the processes of growth, rest, decay and death, we can learn a lot about human processes. It is important to be able to read the soil symbolically and look for personal metaphors in what soil does. This requires time and patience. Slow down, breathe and just observe. It can surprise us in many ways if we work with it instead of trying to control it.

- Often our planting fails but the soil offers itself again for new ideas. The wonderful message from the soil is that it endlessly allows us to fail and continuously gives us a second chance. Failure is never an end in and of itself. Everything composts back into the earth to become the nutrition for new life.

Sources

Avary, C.G., *The Biophilia Effect*, Colorado: Sounds True, 2018.

Braden, G., *The Divine Matrix*, California: Hay House, 2007.

Kimmerer, R.W., *Braiding Sweetgrass*, USA: Penguin Books, 2013.

Li, Q., Morimoto, K., Kobayashi, M., Inagaki, H., Katsumata, M., Hirata, Y., Hirata, K., Suzuki, H., Li, Y.J., Wakayama, Y., Kawanda, T., Park, B.J., Ohira, T., Matsui, N., Kagawa, T., Miyazaki, Y., and Krensky, A.M., 'Visiting a Forest, but Not a City, Increases Human Natural Killer Activity and Expression of Anti-Cancer Proteins', *International Journal of Immunopathology and Pharmacology*, 2008, 21 (1), pp. 117–27.

Li, Q., *Shinrin-Yoku: The Art and Science of Forest-Bathing*, USA: Penguin Books, 2018.

Morita, E., Fukuda, S., Nagano, J., Hamajima, N., Yamamoto, H., Iwai, Y., Nakashima, T., Ohira, T., and Shirakawa, T.J.P.H., 'Psychological effects of forest environments on healthy adults: Shinrin-yoku (forest-air bathing, walking) as a possible method of stress reduction', *Public Health*, 2007, 121 (1), pp. 54–63.

Münzel, T., Schmidt, F.P., Steven, S., Herzog, J., Daiber, A., and Sørensen, M., 'Environmental Noise and the Cardiovascular System', *Journal of the American College of Cardiology*, 2018, 71 (6), pp. 688–97.

Ohlson, K., *The Soil Will Save Us*, New York: Rodale, 2014.

Park, B.J., Tsunetsugu, Y., Kasetani, T., Hirano, H., Kagawa, T., Sato, M., and Miyazaki, Y., 'Physiological Effects of Shinrin-yoku (Taking in the Atmosphere of the Forest) – Using Salivary Cortisol and Cerebral Activity as Indicators', *Journal of Physiological Anthropology*, 2007, 26 (2), pp. 123–8.

Reynolds, M., *The Garden Awakening*, Cambridge: Green Books, 2016.

Roe, J., Thompson, C., Aspinall, P., Brewer, M., Duff, E., Miller, D., Mitchell, R., and Clow, A., 'Green Space and Stress: Evidence from Cortisol Measures in Deprived Urban Communities', *International Journal of Environmental Research and Public Health*, 2013, 10 (9), pp. 4086–103.

Rook, G., 'The Background to the Old Friends Hypothesis', *Grahamrook.net*, http://www.grahamrook.net/OldFriends/oldfriends.html

Selhub, E.M. and Logan, A.C., *Your Brain On Nature*, Toronto: HarperCollins, 2014.

Stuart-Smith, S., *The Well Gardened Mind*, London: William Collins, 2020.

Taylor, R., 'Fractal Patterns in Nature and Art are Aesthetically Pleasing and Stress-reducing', *The Conversation*, 31 March 2017, https://theconversation.com/fractal-patterns-in-nature-and-art-are-aesthetically-pleasing-and-stress-reducing-73255

Ulrich, R., 'View through a window may influence recovery from surgery', *Science*, 1984, 224 (4647), pp. 420–1.

Ulrich, R.S., Simons, R.F., Losito, B.D., Fiorito, E., Miles, M.A., and Zelson, M., 'Stress Recovery During Exposure to Natural and Urban Environments', *Journal of Environmental Psychology*, 1991, 11 (3), pp. 201–30.

Van Den Berg, A.E. and Custers, M.H., 'Gardening promotes neuroendocrine and affective restoration from stress', *Journal of Health Psychology*, 2011, 16 (1), pp. 3–11.

Williams, F., *The Nature Fix*, New York: W.W. Norton, 2018.

Wohlleben, P., *The Hidden Life of Trees*, London: William Collins, 2016.

World Health Organization, *Burden of disease from environmental noise: Quantification of healthy life years lost in Europe*, World Health Organization: Regional Office for Europe, 2011.

Yamaguchi, M., Deguchi, M., and Miyazaki, Y., 'The Effects of Exercise in Forest and Urban Environments on Sympathetic Nervous Activity of Normal Young Adults', *Journal of International Medical Research*, 2006, 34 (2), pp. 152–9.

For more information on green therapy, visit www.greentherapy.ie.